Henry O´Reilly

American civil war. Memories of incidents connected with the Rebellion including the proposition made in November, 1861, when Gen. J. Cochrane advocated the arming of the slaves

Henry O´Reilly

American civil war. Memories of incidents connected with the Rebellion including the proposition made in November, 1861, when Gen. J. Cochrane advocated the arming of the slaves

ISBN/EAN: 9783337207786

Printed in Europe, USA, Canada, Australia, Japan

Cover: Foto ©ninafisch / pixelio.de

More available books at **www.hansebooks.com**

PRICE TEN CENTS.

CHRONICLES

OF

THE REBELLION

OF

1861,

FORMING A

Complete History of the Secession Movement

FROM ITS COMMENCEMENT,

TO WHICH ARE ADDED THE

MUSTER ROLL OF THE UNION ARMY,

AND

EXPLANATORY AND ILLUSTRATIVE NOTES OF THE LEADING FEATURES OF THE CAMPAIGN.

BY CHARLES J. ROSS.

SOLD BY ALL BOOKSELLERS AND NEWSDEALERS.

New-York:

FRANK McELROY, PRINTER, 113 NASSAU STREET.

1861.

BUSINESS NOTICES.

CHRONICLES

OF

THE REBELLION

OF

1861,

FORMING A

Complete History of the Secession Movement

FROM ITS COMMENCEMENT,

TO WHICH ARE ADDED THE

MUSTER ROLL OF THE UNION ARMY,

AND

EXPLANATORY AND ILLUSTRATIVE NOTES OF THE
LEADING FEATURES OF THE CAMPAIGN.

BY CHARLES J. ROSS.

———————•◦•————————

New-York:

FRANK McELROY, PRINTER, 113 NASSAU STREET.

1861.

Chronicles of the Rebellion of 1861.

INTRODUCTION.

THE events connected with the Secession movements of the Southern States, and which roused the people of the North American continent to the highest state of political excitement, will be long held in remembrance. The spectacle of a people so happy and prosperous—living under a Constitution which it was their pride and boast to regard as the most glorious under the sun—a Constitution which, from the expansive character of its principles and provisions, conferred upon its citizens a greater amount of political power, and secured to them a larger extent of civil and religious liberty, than the subjects of any other government—republican or monarchical—plunged into all the dire calamities, the horrors and the sufferings of *Civil War*, is painful in the extreme. But the ultimate result must be beneficial to the country at large. Although its commercial progress may be arrested in its onward career, and the development of its agricultural, manufacturing and mineral resources, for a time be neglected, the Constitution and laws will come out of the fiery ordeal purged and purified of every corruption which time has attached to the governmental system of the United States.

The patriot, the philanthropist, and the statesman, will dwell with feelings of attention and interest upon each and every phase of the great struggle, and from their careful study be more than ever convinced of the greatness and supreme excellence of the federal government and the legislative enactments framed and promulgated for its conduct and guidance. The form of a republican government will meet with a more general sanction, and the dynasties of the old world be taught to entire conviction that "*vox populi*" is "*vox Dei*." Moreover, stript of all the vague plausibilities and metaphysical subtleties put forth by the Secessionists, it will be clearly and indisputably demonstrated that the contest of 1861, between the North and the South, must be regarded as a quarrel between civil and religious liberty on the one hand, and political despotism of the blackest character on the other.

For a long series of years the leading statesmen among the Secessionists planned their grand scheme of treason to the United States. South Carolina took the lead in fomenting rebellion. To put forth an apparent justification of Secession, her leading politicians trumped up charges against the people of the Free States, imputed dishonest and bloodthirsty motives to Northern citizens, and boldly avowed that their designs were nothing less than robbing them of their political rights, destroying their domestic institution—*slavery*—and treating the Southern States as a subjugated province. For these reasons, the facts and incidents of the struggle, from first to last, must be interesting to every one who has the least pretension to patriotism, and desires to be thoroughly posted on the affairs of the country. Their faithful narration in the following pages will prove useful to every one who bestows upon them even a cursory perusal, causing them to be carefully preserved for consultation and reference in after years.

In discharging the duties which we have undertaken, we will strictly adhere to facts, and, should we be led to use occasionally expressions apparently harsh, it will not be from any desire to vilify the

Southern Secessionists, but simply because the stern realities of the exciting period of which we write, and the political iniquity of the revolters, demand that we should be candid, and exhibit in all its criminal deformity the conduct of a misguided people, who have placed the country in social jeopardy, rendered it unprosperous, and, for a time, banished peace and happiness from the land. Although somewhat unwilling to drag in the question of slavery in the discussion of the several topics involved in the subject matter of this volume, we cannot render our task complete without a reference thereto. We shall, however, be as moderate as possible upon a point so peculiarly tender, as the merits of that great question will allow.

CHAPTER I.

THE POSITION OF THE PRO AND ANTI-SLAVERY PARTIES SET FORTH.

That the troubles of 1861 resulted in the wide-spread difference of opinion and the political animosity and enmity engendered thereby, on the subject of free and compulsory labor—in other words, slavery—cannot be disputed. In all the platforms which have been adopted at National or State conventions it has been more or less brought forward. Both parties—Democrat and Republican—have been alike at fault—if a constant agitation of the question merits blame—for each made reference thereto, and contended for the supremacy of their respective views in the preambles and resolves adopted as their platforms. For the better understanding of the position [assumed by the Secessionists, it will not be out of place to notice in detail the principles set forth in all the national platforms adopted for the last twenty years.

In the year 1839, the Abolitionists held a convention at Warsaw, N. Y., for the purpose of endeavoring to elect as president of the United States, a candidate favorable to abolition principles, and resolved that, in its judgment, "every consideration of duty and expediency which ought to control the action of Christian freemen, requires of the Abolitionists of the United States to organize a distinct and independent political party, embracing all necessary means for nominating candidates for office, and sustaining them by public suffrage." The gentlemen elected by this convention for president and vice-president, declined the proposed honor, and the party was unsuccessful in its first effort on behalf of abolitionism. The attitude assumed by the Convention assembled at Warsaw brought out a strong opposition to the sentiments adopted in reference to the slavery question. Accordingly the Democratic National Convention, which met at Baltimore on the 5th of May, 1840, resolved, "that all efforts by Abolitionists or others made to induce Congress to interfere with the question of slavery, or take incipient steps in relation thereto, are calculated to lead to dangerous and alarming consequences, and that all such efforts have a tendency to diminish the happiness of the people, and endanger the stability and permanency of the Union." Thus, for the first time did the Abolitionists and Pro-slavery parties join issue upon that grand proposition—the agitation of which in no small degree brought about the perilous and troubled times of which we write— "the power of Congress under the Constitution to interfere with or control the domestic institutions of the several States, such States being the sole and proper judges of everything pertaining to their own affairs, not prohibited by the Constitution."

It is, however, worthy of remark, that the grand movers in the rebellion of 1861 manifested a dislike of federal authority and control, as the nullification schemes put forth by South Carolina and Virginia in 1832 and 1833 plainly attest. Thanks to the fidelity and decision of Gen. Jackson, the then project of disunion was nipped in the bud, and hence the change of tactics adopted at the Baltimore Convention first quoted. They had learned to fear the influence and power of the Northern Democracy, and as they could not successfully carry out a policy of open assault against it and the Union, the expedient of sapping and mining both was determined upon. In this we have a key to the motives which induced Mr. Calhoun, and politicians of his school, to join the regular democratic party in 1837—a party which they abhorred and openly stigmatized for the four previous years. The inspired writings contain an injunction: "Be ye wise as serpents but harmless as doves." This the original Secessionists imitated with no small success.

When they made their way into the councils of the National Democratic party, which, as already noted, took place in 1837, they lost no time in putting into operation such schemes as would enable them to carry out their original designs. Like Homœopathic physicians, they commenced by administering small doses, in fact, merely preparing the constitution of that body politic for the great *denouement* which they had in view. At the outset they confined themselves to the simple modification of the Democratic party, but subsequently remodeled it more and more in harmony with their peculiar ideas and principles.

These are not vague assertions. The history of the Democratic party from the year 1837 until 1860, affords innumerable proofs of the accuracy of our statements. Suffice it at present to say that the war with Mexico and the annexation of Texas were results arising from the " pursuit of aims purely Southern and sectional," that " it was to subserve Southern, and eventually all disunion purposes, that the Missouri Compromise was repealed, and all the evil energy of Lecomptonism put into operation."*

But to return to the National Conventions. We find that the Abolitionists in 1843, under a new name—the Liberal party—met at Buffalo on the 30th of August, and there proclaimed, that " the Liberal party has not been organized merely for the overthrow of slavery; its first decided effort must indeed be directed against slaveholding—as the grossest and most revolting manifestations of despotism." And again, they also declared, and " gave it to be distinctly understood by this nation and the world, that, as Abolitionists, considering that the strength of our cause lies in its righteousness, and our hope for it in conformity to the laws of God and our respect for the RIGHTS OF MAN, we owe it to the Sovereign Ruler of the universe, as a proof of our allegiance to him, in all our civil relations and offices, whether as private citizens or as public functionaries, sworn to support the Constitution of the United States, to regard and treat the third clause of the fourth article of that instrument, whenever applied to the case of a fugitive slave, as utterly null and void, and, consequently, as forming no part of the Constitution of the United States, whenever we are called upon or

* Partisan Leader.

sworn to support it."* This was, no doubt, strong language, and well calculated to irritate the people of the South. The Convention, however, deemed it proper to put forth an apologetic reason for its adoption, and therefore declared " that the peculiar patronage and support hitherto extended to slavery and slaveholding by the general government ought to be immediately withdrawn, and the example of national influence and authority ought to be arrayed on the side of liberty and free labor."

The next great " platform" was that adopted at the Free Democratic Convention in 1848. This body admitted the right of the slave owners to manage their own affairs as they pleased, and contended that " Congress has no more right to make a slave than make a king; no more power to institute or establish slavery, than to establish monarchy; no such power can be found among those specifically conferred by the Constitution, or derived by just implication from them." The object of this resolution was to frustrate the designs of the Southern party, who, at this time, were wielding considerable influence, not only in the National Conventions and Congress, but in a great degree monopolizing all the important and lucrative positions in the gift of the national government. Passing on to 1852, we find the Whig party acquiescing in the provisions of the slave law, and their candidate, Gen. Scott, declaring that he was " convinced that harmony or good-will between the different quarters of our broad country is essential to the present and the future interest of the Republic, that can know no North and no South." He then adds : " I should neither countenance nor tolerate any sedition, disorder, faction, or resistance to the laws of the Union, on any pretext, in any part of the land." Little did this great man think, when he gave expression to such patriotic sentiments, that nine years afterwards he would be called upon to do the very thing he somewhat obscurely foreshadowed—put down " sedition, disorder, faction, and resistance to the law of the Union." It was the promulgation of this sentiment which rendered Gen. Scott odious in the

* The fourth article of the Constitution of the United States reads thus : " The United States shall guarantee to every State in this Union a republican form of government, and shall protect each of them against invasion, and on application of the legislature or of the executive (where the legislature cannot be convened), against domestic violence."

eyes of the Southerners. When they should maturely hatch their schemes of rebellion, they well knew that, if living, he would be the man whose military genius would thwart them in their designs. It is worthy of remark that the declaration of such Liberal principles, coming from the liberal party—the advocates of free labor—did not tally with the accusation so often made by the Southern leaders, that the North sought to override the South. Notwithstanding the high prestige of Gen. Scott, he was unsuccessful. A man so firm and determined in his purposes, and patriotic and liberal in his principles, was not likely to find favor in the eyes of a party who for a long series of years had used every exertion to carry into effect a political policy exactly the opposite. Accordingly, the Democratic Convention, held at Baltimore in 1852, took its stand upon the principle that "Congress has no power, under the Constitution, to interfere with or control the domestic institutions of the several States, and that such States are the sole and proper judges of everything appertaining to their own affairs, and prohibited by the Constitution: that all efforts of the Abolitionists or others, made to induce Congress to interfere with questions of slavery, or to take incipient steps in relation thereto, are calculated to lead to the most alarming and dangerous consequences, and that all such efforts have an inevitable tendency to diminish the happiness of the people, and endanger the stability and permanency of the Union, and ought to be discountenanced by any friend of our political union." This resolution is nearly word for word with the one passed at the Democratic Convention in the same city twelve years previously. But the position of the slavery question was quite different in 1852 from what it was in 1840.

The year 1850 brought about what is known as the "Missouri Compromise." A measure such as this was well calculated to call forth keen and acrimonious debates. Of course it was to be expected that Senators and Representatives from slaveholding States would oppose such restrictions as this measure intended to enforce. It abridged slavery extension, and took from its advocates one of the main props by which they hoped to support their grand idea of throwing off the yoke of allegiance to the United States, becoming their own masters, and

carrying slavery into every nook and corner of the territorial possessions of the Union. The discussions which took place on the "Missouri Compromise" clearly showed that, notwithstanding the desire of the Northern States to do everything which could reasonably be expected of them, and to appease the unbrotherly feeling of the Southerners, the concessions then made were only the precursor to other and more unreasonable commands.

Allusion has been made to the platform of the Democratic Convention at Baltimore, in 1852. At this time a feeling began to pervade a certain class of politicians, who, although swayed by Democratic tendencies, felt that they could not endorse the proclivities of the South to the extent that was demanded of them. They accordingly formed themselves into a free Democratic Convention, met at Pittsburg on the 11th of August, and adopted a platform. Its declaration of principles and measures are remarkable for boldness of position and firmness of purpose. We quote the following in confirmation of this opinion:

"That the Constitution of the United States, ordained to form a more perfect union, to establish justice, and to secure the blessings of liberty, expressly denies to the general government all power to deprive any person of life, liberty, or property, without due process of law: and, therefore, the government having no more power to establish slavery than to establish a monarchy, should at once proceed to relieve itself from all responsibility for the existence of slavery, whenever it possesses constitutional power to legislate for its extinction. That to the persevering and importunate demands of the slave power for more slave States, new slave territories, and the nationalization of slavery, our distinct and final answer is—No more slave States, no slave territory, no nationalized slavery, and no national legislation for the extradition of slaves. That slavery is a sin against God, and a crime against man, which no human enactment nor usuage can make right, and that Christianity, humanity, and patriotism, alike demand its abolition. That the Fugitive Slave Act of 1850 is repugnant to the Constitution, to the principles of the common law, to the spirit of Christianity, and to the sentiments of the civilized world; we, therefore, deny its binding force upon the

American people, and demand its immediate and total repeal."*

The promulgation of such doctrines, couched in such strong language, and advocated and endorsed by the leading men of all the free States, must have shown the slaveholders of the South that their political influence and reign of what had been regarded as semi-tyranny, was drawing to a close. The Democratic wing of the country had become split upon the slavery question. And it only required time to bring about an opportunity for testing at the polls whether the government of the United States was to be carried on in accordance with the principles and provisions of the Constitution, or the dictates of a party who had for years squelched public opinion on the question of the immoral and anti-Christian character of slavery.

The questions involved in the "Missouri Compromise" were brought up by the Republican National Convention, which met at Philadelphia on the 17th of June, 1856. This body resolved, "That the Constitution confers upon Congress sovereign power over the territories of the United States for their government, and that in the exercise of this power, it is both the right and the duty of Congress to prohibit in the territories these twin relics of barbarism—Polygamy and Slavery." To counteract the effectual application of the principle just quoted, the Democratic National Convention assembled at Cincinnati, and drafted and adopted that celebrated document called the "Cincinnati Platform," the convention pledging itself to "resist all attempts of renewing in Congress, or out of it, the agitation of the slavery question under whatever shape or color the attempt may be made." The decided opinions of the two conventions just referred to, brought out a third party, the result of which was the assembling of a Whig National Convention at Baltimore, on the 17th of September, 1856. The object of this organization was to elect a President from among the politicians of that day, a man who would cast aside the peculiar dogmas and doctrines held by the respective geographical sections of the country, at the time arrayed in political antagonism. Mr. Fillmore was their nominee, but Mr. Buchanan being put forward by the Cincinnati Convention, carried the day. Here we shall not

* See Political Text Book for 1861, page 21.

enter into any remarks upon the conduct and policy of the Buchanan administration. It will, however form the subject for serious reflection and lengthened observation in another part of this work.

The preceding remarks bring us down to the last Presidential campaign. In the year 1859, and the early part of 1860, a somewhat universal opinion prevailed that so strong was the Abolition sentiment in the Northern States, aided, as it had been, by the insane attempt of John Brown and his misguided followers to seize and hold Harper's Ferry, that the time had come to meet and avert it. In connection, with this feeling, the publication of the "Impending Crisis," or "Irrepressible Conflict," had no small share in influencing and inflaming the minds of Southern citizens. Consequently, when the time had arrived for holding national conventions, for adopting platforms, and nominating candidates for President and Vice-President, there was strong feeling among all parties. At the very outset it was evident that the great struggle would eventuate in the maintenance or non-existence of the Union. The republicans met at Chicago on the 16th of May, 1860, and at once proclaimed that "the new dogma that the Constitution, of its own force, carries slavery into all or any of the territories of the United States, is a dangerous political heresy, at variance with the explicit provisions of that instrument itself, with contemporaneous exposition, and with legislative and judicial precedent, is revolutionary in its tendencies, and subversive of the peace and harmony of the country." The result of this convention was the nomination and subsequent election of Mr. Lincoln as President, and Mr. Hamlin as Vice-President. Three weeks previous to this the Democratic party met at Charleston, S. C. This convention was composed of very discordant materials. How could it be otherwise, after the declaration of the Democratic Free-Soil Convention already alluded to? The great bone of contention was the slavery issue. Northern Democrats were quite aware of the strength of the Republican party, and could not, therefore, fall in with, much less endorse or approve of the bold ideas broached in the speeches of Messrs. Avery, Howell Cobb, A. H. Stephens, &c., &c. The sentiments of these gentlemen clearly indicated that, unless they could control the presidential election, they would attempt to carry out the idea which many of them had not only professed, but positively advocated and expounded within the walls of Congress. After days of fruitless discussion, the Southern States perceiving that they would be outvoted, began to "protest" and withdraw from the convention. Alabama, Mississippi, South Carolina, Florida, Texas, Arkansas, Georgia, and Lousiana followed each other in quick succession. Reasons as plenty as blackberries in September were put forth by each delegation, as it was about to make its final bow to the Democratic Convention. When they bade "adieu," they understood each other so far that they would break the back-bone of the Northern Democracy, but foolishly omitting to reflect that, by so doing, they were only playing into the hands of their political opponents, the Republicans. They ultimately held an adjourned meeting at Richmond, Va., and, after much political manœuvering, they, with some more seceding States, fixed their choice of nomination upon Breckinridge and Lane, for President and Vice-President. Those who remained firm at Charleston, seeing the aspect of affairs at their early sittings, adjourned to meet at Baltimore. Here fresh defections took place, resulting in a confirmation of the nomination of Breckinridge and Lane. Meantime, the delegates met at Baltimore, and continued their deliberations until Stephen A Douglas and Herschel V. Johnson were nominated as the regular Democratic candidates for President and Vice-President.

We must not omit to state that the meeting of the Democratic Convention at Charleston was somewhat remarkable, from the fact that the New-York delegation, under the peculiar auspices of the Hon. Fernando Wood, was denied a seat, or any participation in the deliberations which ensued. That the delegates of a party, headed by such a man (for without endorsing any one of his political objects or ideas, we have no hesitation in stating our belief, that he is one of the foremost politicians of the age, and that he has few equals in the argumentation of any subject relating to national or State policy) should be excluded, is not only wonderful, but serves to show that there was, even in the Democratic camp, a strong feeling to put an end to the tyrannical designs of the South.

In the position of affairs just noted, the reader will perceive that there were now

before the public three distinct candidates for the office of President, and a like number for that of Vice-President. It had occurred to many deep and reflecting minds that some efforts should be made to thwart the designs of those who would destroy the union of the United States. Accordingly, a convention of delegates, coming from twenty States, and claiming to represent the Constitutional party, met at Baltimore on the 29th of May, and nominated for President John Bell, of Tennessee; and for Vice-President Edward Everett, of Massachusetts. The principles adopted in the platform of this convention included the doctrine that it is the part of patriotism, and of duty, to recognize no political principle other than the Constitution of the country, the Union of the States, and the enforcement of the laws. They further resolved, "That, as representatives of the Constitutional men of the country, in National Convention assembled, we hereby pledge ourselves to maintain, protect, and defend, separately and unitedly, those great principles of public liberty and national safety against all enemies at home and abroad." In principles such as these every man could unite. Subsequent events showed that had Bell and Everett been placed in office the rebellion of 1861, if not altogether averted, would have been for a series of years postponed.

CHAPTER II.

THE SAME SUBJECT CONTINUED.

HAVING glanced at the political doctrines enumerated in the "platforms" of the conventions of all the leading political parties, from 1840 to 1860, we proceed to notice the opinions and principles put forth in the letters and speeches of the more prominent candidates for the offices of President and Vice-President. The first to which we would call attention are the sentiments of the Hon. Daniel Webster. In the United States Senate in August, 1848, he thus expressed himself, in speaking on the bill to organize the territory of Oregon, with a clause prohibiting slavery: "The question now is, whether it is competent to Congress, in the exercise of a fair and just discretion, to say that there have been five slaveholding States—Louisiana,

Florida, Arkansas, Missouri, and Texas —added to the Union out of foreign acquisitions, and as yet only one free State; whether, under this state of things, it is unreasonable and unjust, in the slightest degree, to limit their further extension. As to the power of Congress, I have nothing to add to what I said the other day. I have said that I shall not consent to the extension of slavery on this continent, nor any increase of slave representation in the other house of Congress." Ten years before this, Mr. Millard Fillmore, in his Buffalo Letter, as it is termed, in reply to an inquiry by the Anti-Slavery Committee of the county of Erie, stated that he was of opinion that petitions to Congress, on the subject of slavery and the slave trade, ought to be received, read, and respectfully considered by the representatives of the people; that he was opposed to the annexation of Texas, under any circumstance, so long as slaves were held therein. He also stated that he was in favor of immediate legislation for the abolition of slavery in the District of Columbia. This same gentleman, nearly twenty years later—1856—foresaw what was about to happen to this country; for we find him speaking in very severe terms of censure of a political party presenting candidates for the Presidency and Vice-Presidency, selected from the free States alone, with the avowed purpose of electing these candidates by sufferance of one part of the Union only, to rule over the whole of the United States. Conduct such as this, Mr. Fillmore predicted, would bring about civil war, and time has led to the realization of his unpleasant anticipations.

But to come down to the period immediately preceding the secession of the Southern States, we find Mr. Lincoln, in accepting the nomination for President, agreeing to all the principles put forth by the Chicago platform. He furthermore pledged himself to respect the rights of all the States and territories, and people of the nation, to the inviolability of the Constitution, and the perpetual union, harmony, and prosperity of all. The opponents of Mr. Lincoln, particularly those residing in the Southern States, have accused him of endorsing the work of Helper, entitled the "Irrepressible Conflict." Let us examine more closely his views upon the subject of slavery. In the course of his address at the Cooper Union, on the 27th of February, 1860, he stated: "Human action can be modified to some extent, but human nature cannot be changed. There is a judgment and feeling against slavery in this nation, which cast at least a million and a half of votes." Again, "An inspection of the Constitution will show that the right of property in a slave is not distinctly and expressly affirmed in it. Bear in mind, the judges do not pledge their judicial opinion that such right is implicitly affirmed in the Constitution; but they pledge their veracity that it is distinctly and expressly affirmed there, that is, not mingled with anything else—'expressly,' that is, in words just meaning that, without the aid of any inference, and susceptible of no other meaning." There is a good deal of special pleading in all this, but toward the close of his address he expressed principles and sentiments of the most moderate character. "Even though," he said, "the Southern people will not so much as listen to us, let us calmly consider their demand and yield to them, if in our deliberate view of our duty we can possibly do so. Judging by all they say and do, and by the subject and nature of their controversy with us, let us determine, if we can, what will satisfy them." In all this there is not a single word which could lead the South to anticipate any evil result from Mr. Lincoln's elevation to the White House. Nor was there anything offensive said towards the States which seceded in the Chicago platform, upon which his election was carried. It is true that the slavery question was condemned, but the language adopted was pretty much the same as was used by the Abolitionists twenty years before. Moreover, Mr. Lincoln's inaugural address plainly showed that he was determined to administer the government without "favor, affection, or ill-will" to any one. How far he has performed that obligation of his office, every one acquainted with the passing events of the day can form a correct opinion. For ourselves, we consider he acted up to all his promises and professions with great exactitude, and not without success. Mr. Hamlin, the Vice-President, is of kindred feelings and sentiments on all the great questions of the day. Nothing appears in the political records which would warrant the South to take umbrage at him as President of the Senate, and even the premier, Mr.

Seward, has given evidence that much as he may dislike slavery, he is prepared to concede to the South all her just rights. and to allow her to manage her domestic concerns as interest and taste may dictate.

Turning from the Republican party we would next glance at the sentiments and expressions of the Democratic candidates. Mr. Breckenridge, in accepting the nomination, writes strongly in favor of slave property, and significantly hints that " it has been necessary, more than once, to pause and solemnly assert the true character of this government." Gen. Lane, in his letter of acceptance, adopts as his creed—" Non-intervention on the subject of slavery, non-intervention by Congress, and non-intervention by territorial legislators;" contending that " if the Constitution establishes the right of every citizen to enter the common territory with whatever property he legally possesses, it necessarily devolves on the Federal Government to protect the right of the citizen whenever or wherever assailed or infringed." The General made some slight allusions to the beneficial effect arising from the success of his party, as we might then expect an era of peace and harmony. Failing that, the inference is clear that the South had made up its mind to revolt from the United States. Senator Douglas, who has paid the great debt of nature, and whose loss the country at the present time so much deplores, in his letter of acceptation of nomination for the presidency, laid down the doctrine, that the peace of the country and the perpetuity of the Union had been put in jeopardy by attempts to interfere with and control the domestic affairs of the people in the territories, through the agency of the Federal Government. He proclaimed himself an earnest and zealous advocate for non-intervention, by Congress, with slavery in the territories. Notwithstanding his decided opinions, Mr. Douglas was a Union-loving man. The Constitutional Union candidates, Bell and Everett, were strongly in favor of the Union. The former ratted—proved himself a political apostate, and sold himself to the cause of disunion and treason. Mr. Everett still clings to the Union, and is faithful to his political creed. Among the many able writers and speakers in defence of the Union, there are none who have so argumentatively and eloquently demonstrated that the course adopted by

the South was illegal and immoral in the highest degree.

From the time of holding the National Conventions in May and June, 1860, until the day of election in the November following, the campaign was carried on with much spirit on both sides. The Pro-slavery party were loth to declare their intentions as to treason and rebellion, should Mr. Lincoln carry the day. The worst passions were exhibited during the contest, and every artifice was resorted to for the purpose of blackening the public character of the Republican candidates in the eyes of the citizens at large. It should be observed that the Southern States for several years had been in the habit of controling the government, and thereby obtaining the lion's share of the spoils of office. To lose these spoils, and to be shorn of their political prestige, combined with their fanciful anticipation of evil at the hands of a Republican government, almost drove them mad, and long before Mr. Lincoln's election was an accomplished fact, the leaders of South Carolina made up their mind to take leave of the United States, and set up a government of their own. No promise nor asseveration, be it ever so serious, was of the least avail. The prosperity of the North was to them a great source of annoyance. They coveted a direct European trade, and out of a dissolution of the Union they believed they would realize this grand commercial benefit.

We have now taken a brief review of the men and parties for the last thirty years, and from it perceived that the main element of agitation has been the slavery question : and that some of our greatest men have decidedly opposed slavery extension, while others were restless in the agitation of measures designed to foster and perpetuate the "domestic institution" of the South: We have also observed that, so long as the South could control the North in the Federal Government of the country, their threats of secession were not heard, but instantly the Republican party got the upper hand, that moment they became restless and ungovernable.

CHAPTER III.

SOUTHERN TACTICS IN THE LATTER END OF 1860.

FROM the tone adopted by the Southern leaders at the Charleston Convention, it

was evident that the election of a Republican president would be merely the fore-
runner of secession. This was quite clear
from the language adopted in the protests
of the delegates of the several Southern
States, as they withdrew from the convention. A few extracts from some of the
addresses will prove our position. Mr.
Glenn, of Mississippi, told the convention :
" The South leaves you—not like Hagar,
driven into the wilderness, friendless and
alone—but I tell Southern men here, and
for them, I tell the North, that in less
than sixty days you will find a united
South standing side by side with us. Let
me say to you, that the time may come
when you will need us more than we need
you. There slumbers in your midst a
latent spark, not of political sectionalism,
but of social discord, which may yet require the conservative principles of the
South to save your region of the country
from anarchy and confusion. We need
not your protection. The power of the
Black Republicans is nothing to us. We
are safe in our own strength and security,
as long as we maintain our rights." The
protest from the Texas delegates set forth
that—" if the principles of the Northern
Democracy are properly represented by
the opinion and action of the majority of
the delegates from that section on this
floor, we do not hesitate to declare, that
their principles are not only not ours, but,
if adhered to and enforced by them, will
destroy this Union." The Arkansas delegation was equally emphatic in its protest,
alleging that the " violation of plighted
faith on the part of the numerical majority—this violation of the well-established
usage and custom of the party—drive us to
the conclusion, that we cannot longer
safely trust the fortunes of slaveholding
States to the chances of the numerical
majority, in a convention where all the
Black Republicans of the Union—the im-
mense populations of Massachusetts, New-
York, Pennsylvania, and Ohio, and other
Northern States — are fully represented
on the one side, against the small populations of the slave States on the other.
Had these populations adhered strictly
to the usages and customs of the party,
longer association might have been prac-
ticable ; but annihilation is staring us in
the face, and we are admonished of our
duty to stand upon our rights." The entire of the Southern discontents drew
up their protests in tone and sentiment
pretty similar. All, more or less, threat-

ened that if their opinion upon Democratic doctrines and principles were not
conceded, the Union was in danger.

No sooner had it become a positive
fact that Mr. Lincoln would be elected,
than South Carolina set about calling a
State Convention, for the purpose of
throwing off its allegiance to the United
States ; and months before the time for
Mr. Lincoln assuming the responsibilities
of office at the White House, the Secession Ordinance was passed, and other
States invited to follow the example set by
South Carolina. The convention which
drew up the Secession Ordinance of South
Carolina also put forth a declaration of
causes which induced their political action. Among other statements contained in
this document we find the following : " We
assert that fourteen of the States have
deliberately refused for years past to fulfil
their Constitutional obligations, and we
refer to their own statutes for the proof."
The matter to which allusion is here
made is to the Fugitive Slave Law, and
charges the several free States with desiring to discharge fugitives from the service of labor claimed, inasmuch as in
none of them had the State government
complied with the stipulation in the
Constitution.* Although the requirements of the Constitution, with regard to
fugitive slaves, are pretty plain, the
wording of the fourth article is open to
disputation and a variety of interpreta-
tion. For example, the wording of the
article endows the slave with *personality*,
whereas the Slave Code as positively denies such a quality to slaves held to
labor. In the foot-notes of Mr. W. Good-
ell's " National Charters for the Million,"
there is an interesting argument against
claims of slaveholders, with regard to
the rendition of their fugive slaves. He
says :

" The history, as well as the words of
this clause, forbids its application to
fugitive slaves. Towards the close of the
convention a proposal was made to insert
a provision for reclaiming fugitive slaves.
It was scouted by general approbation,
and abandoned without defence. The
next day *this* clause, concerning " per-

* The fourth article of the Constitution runs in these
words : " No person held to service or labor in any
State, under the laws thereof, escaping into another,
shall, in consequence of any law or regulation therein,
be discharged from such service or labor, but shall be
delivered up, on claim of the party to whom such service or labor may be due."

sons" from whom service or labor may be due, was proposed and unanimously adopted, without debate. So that the indignant refusal of the convention to provide for the rendition of fugitive slaves is an established historical fact."

Before going into a narrative of the subsequent acts of Jefferson Davis and his party, up to the evacuation of Fort Sumter, we pause to take a brief review of the ground already gone over, and especially to notice the singular political corruptions of the Democratic party during the administration of Mr. Buchanan. In the consideration of the facts brought out in the report of the Covode investigation, it will be borne in mind that the President of the United States, Mr. Buchanan, submitted to the House of Representatives a protest against the authority and right to take cognizance of the matters which the committee proposed to investigate. The fact of this step upon the part of Mr. Buchanan raised, in the minds of the Republican members of Congress, a strong opinion that all was not right, and that revelations of a startling and painful character would be brought to light. Evidently Mr. Buchanan assumed a false position in opposing the appointment of the Covode committee. Numbers of precedents existed for its appointment, and exercise of all the powers of inquiry conferred upon it. Commencing with Mr. Mason's motion, in 1826, for a committee to inquire into the expediency of diminishing or regulating the patronage of the executive of the United States, we come to Mr. Calhoun's committee in 1835, for a like purpose. Mr. Houston moved for and obtained a committee in the Senate, in August, 1852, for the investigation of political corruption in matters relating to Congress, or the conduct of the executive. The first part of the Covode investigation was the conduct of Mr. Buchanan and his cabinet, on the Lecompton Constitution. The report of the Committee thus speaks of that conduct: "The patriot will mourn, the historian will pause with astonishment over this shameless record. Accustomed as the American people are to the errors and crimes of those in power, they will read this exposure with feelings of unmingled indignation." The committee then proceed to summarize the facts revealed by the testimony. For the information of the reader, and in order to more clearly illustrate the tactics of the Southern slave-

owners, we shall append the committee's conviction, as given in the report.*

This was a pretty extensive bill of indictment, but any one who peruses the evidence of the several witnesses examined, will at once admit that the Covode committee had strong grounds for laying the sweeping charges which they did at Mr. Buchanan's door. The testimony of Governor Walker is very emphatic upon these points; for, taken in the most favorable light, what does it prove? Simply this: that Mr. Buchanan and his cabinet had not only practised "duplicity and inconsistency, but treachery to himself as a public officer, after they had implored him to accept a perilous and profitless position, and to a principle which they were the first to present to his favor."† What was the object of such reprehensible conduct? Nothing less than a desire to make Kansas a slave State, and that too in defiance of the expressed will of the people therein. But the abuses in some of the public offices throughout the country, showing, as they do, reprehensible and illegal combinations among the federal officers, with a view to control the sentiments and preferences of the people in their primary political movements, and the corrupt employment of the public moneys, &c., in violation of law, and government regulation, to promote the designs and intentions of the Pro-slavery party, are not less remarkable, and worthy of universal condemnation. The employment of political partisans to situations in the public departments of the country, at extravagant salaries, considering that many of them

<hr/>

* First. The emphatic and unmistakable pledges of the President, as well before as after his election, and the pledges of all his cabinet, to the doctrine of leaving the people of Kansas perfectly free to form and regulate their domestic institutions in their own way.

Second. The deliberate violation of this pledge, and the attempt to convert Kansas into a slave State, by means of forgeries, frauds, and force.

Third. The removal, and the attempt to disgrace the sworn agents of the administration, who refused to violate this pledge.

Fourth. The open employment of the public money in the passage of the Lecompton and English bills through the Congress of the United States.

Fifth. The admission of the parties engaged in the work of electioneering these schemes that they received enormous sums for this purpose, and proof in the checks upon which they were paid by an agent of the administration.

Sixth. The offer to purchase newspapers and newspaper editors, by offers of extravagant sums of money.

Seventh. And, finally, the proscription of Democrats of high standing, who would not support the Lecompton and English bills.

† Covode Investigation, p. 7.

were not called upon to discharge scarcely any duties, is to be deprecated at any time, but when the system is adopted for the avowed object of promoting Pro-slavery interests, and stifling the expressed will of the majority of the people, the act becomes criminal in the highest degree. No wonder that the free State party should have arisen in their majesty in November, 1860, and put an end to the reign of that Democracy which had then assumed proportions of political wickedness so formidable that its further endurance was a matter of complete impossibility.

It is only fair to state, that there was what is termed a "minority report" by the Covode Committee. Mr. Buchanan had his interests and views represented thereon. The leader of that section of the Committee was the Hon. Mr. Winslow. He acted more as a retained advocate for Mr. Buchanan than an independent member of the House of Representatives, deputed to enquire into the truth or falsehood of the charges brought against the Federal Executive and his subordinates. Desiring, in the course of this work, to act upon the adage "audi alterem partem," it will not be out of place to notice the propositions and opinions put forth by the "minority." The successful *nisi prius* pleader never fails, when addressing a jury, to endeavor to throw "metaphysical dust" in their mental vision, and, with an unlimited license, stigmatise the cause of his opposing counsel. If facts and figures are against him, if his legal points are untenable, and his case is, what lawyers term *desperate*, his last resort is to indulge in forensic declamation in denouncing the prosecution or the defense, as the case may be, ignoble, unjust, and unmerciful. This would seem to be the part performed by Mr. Winslow. In the "minority report" he began by denouncing the character of the investigation, as it covered so much ground, and opened such an illimitable field for the gratification of personal spleen and malignity. What motives more undignified and unworthy could be imputed? Afterwards most of the witnesses who gave testimony against the administration of Mr. Buchan-

an were termed a "pack of slanderous jackals of society, who are ever barking at the heels of respectability, ank snuffing for their favorite repast—the offals of slandered reputations. The coward sheltered under an anonymous signature could vent all his spleen and malignity without risk of discovery, and the course of the investigation had stimulated informers, and encouraged tale-bearers." Such was the spirit evinced by Mr. Winslow in the introduction of his "minority report." Thus influenced, his first object was to impeach the credibilty of the witnesses. He avered that most of the charges were founded upon "anonymous communications, others upon information from persons destitute of character and without position, displaced office-holders, disappointed office-seekers, venal placemen, adventurers—mercenary Swiss, whose politics were bounded by no loftier motive than interest." The charge respecting the Lecompton Constitution is noticed thus : "If such a charge were true, it might effect the character of the President for candor and fair dealing, but the offence" (forcing upon an unwilling peo ple a Constitution confining their suffrages to the naked question of slavery), "if improper in morals, is not impenetrable in law." Whether the expounders of American Constitutional jurisprudence will agree with this opinion, shall not be here decided. Nevertheless, it has the appearance of novelty, and, if correct, would open the door effectually for the perpetration of those acts of "forgeries, fraud, and force," so emphatically set forth in the "majority report." Mr. Winslow, as any other lawyer would do, exercised his legal ingenuity in making "the worse appear the better cause." His dexterous manœuvre to carry on the investigation during the recess, and thereby postpone the promulgation of the Committee's report until after the Presidential election, was a great political move, and one which, had it been successful, would have wielded no small influence at the election polls in November, 1860. Mr. Winslow failed in his designs. The report was made public just as the Presidential campaign was in full blast, and it expressed most unsparingly what, for sake of distinction, merits the appellation of—the last sins of the Democracy.

The conclusion of Mr. Winslow's report is not less remarkable for the admissions which it makes than for the scurrility which characterized its introduction. He admitted that there were frauds in Pennsylvania, but they are excusable on the ground that they were committed by "both of the great parties." Such an apology for maladministration has rarely, if ever, been put forth; and the people to whom it would be addressed—if acceptable —would show that they were merely political serfs, unfit for the enjoyment of constitutional liberty, and incompetent to exercise all those rights and privileges which appertain to the independent and patriotic citizens of every free and enlightened country. "Irregularities" are acknowledged to have existed in the Navy Yard at Philadelphia, as well as "responsible irregularities" in some of the post offices and custom houses; but all this took place without the concurrence or sanction of the President, or any of his cabinet. Mr. Winslow does not attempt to prove that, therefore, as much importance must be attached to his confident assertions as would be to the feed advocate who contends that his client is not guilty of murder, although the proof is beyond dispute, and the murderer himself has actually told him so before being given in charge to the jury. Admitting the position put forward by Mr. Winslow— namely, that the object of the Covode investigation was to injure the public character of Mr. Buchanan in the estimation of his fellow-citizens, it does not follow that that can in any degree palliate for the political corruption and other governmental misdemeanors, of which the majority of the Covode Committee contend they had ample proof.

To sum up, in a few words, the impression created upon our mind after a perusal of the "Covode Investigation," we must confess is that Mr. Buchanan's administration was carried out, from first to last, for the purpose of extending slavery. The South issued its dictates as a master, sup-ported by national authority, and the North quietly assented to its imperious dictates. New demands were made every day. In quick succession did exaction follow exaction, prostrating, one after the other, all safeguards and securities—the Wilmot Proviso, the Missouri Compromise, the right of majorities in the territories, and the actual sovereignty of the States cast aside by the Dred Scott decision. By means such as these, the slaveholders of the South succeeded in drawing the United States into those violent and dishonest political practices which marked the administration of Mr. Buchanan, and which have been so thoroughly exposed by the "Covode Investigation." We might write a whole volume upon these themes, and show therefrom that the triumph of the Republican party was owing in no small degree to the corrupt conduct of the Buchanan ministry, and the tyrannical demeanor of the slaveholding States. That triumph effected a preconceived design—secession—and with it the inauguration of civil war.

CHAPTER IV.

SECESSION PROGRESS.

To return to the slaveholders of the South. The convention at Charleston passed their famous ordinance of Secession on the 20th day of December, 1860. This first act in the great drama of rebellion was taken up with much enthusiasm, not only in every quarter of South Carolina, but throughout the adjoining Slave States. At Mobile, there was a military parade; one hundred guns were fired; the bells rang merrily; and the people by hundreds perambulated the streets, expressing unbounded satisfaction at the idea of separation from the United States. The enthusiasm was even greater in New Orleans. There, too, one hundred guns were fired, and the pelican flag unfurled. Impromptu secession speeches were delivered by leading citizens, and the "Marseillaise Hymn" and polkas were the only airs sung and played. Tennessee also contributed her quota to the general rejoicing. In a word, all the States which subsequently formed themselves into the "Southern Confederacy" thus early gave manifestations of their approval of the step taken by South Carolina. In the midst of all this agitation and excitement in every region of the Slave Dominion, the Members of Congress for South Carolina took leave of the Senate and House of Representatives, in short but emphatic speeches, indicating firmness of purpose and a determination on the part of South Carolina to defend to the very last extremity the course which had been adopted. Meanwhile, the secession mania had spread with rapidity throughout the South, as may be perceived by a glance at the following tabular statement, showing:

THE PERIODS OF SECESSION OF THE CONFEDERATE STATES.

The disloyal States seceded in the following order:

State.	Date of Secession.	Vote of Convention.
South Carolina....	December 20, 1860....	——
Mississippi........	January 9, 1861......	84 to 15
Alabama..........	January 11, 1861.....	61 to 39
Florida...........	January 11, 1861.....	62 to 7
Georgia...........	January 19, 1861.....	208 to 89
Louisiana.........	January 26, 1861.....	113 to 17
Texas.............	February 1, 1861......	166 to 7
Virginia..........	April 17, 1861........	
Arkansas..........	May 6, 1861..........	69 to 1

DATE OF RATIFICATION OF THE CONFEDERATE STATES CONSTITUTION.

These States have ratified the Constitution of the Confederate States by the following pole:

State.	Date of Ratification.	Vote of Convention.
Alabama..........	March 13, 1861..	87 to 5
Georgia	March 16, 1861..	96 to 5
Louisiana........	March 21, 1861..	101 to 7
Texas	March 25, 1861..	68 to 2
Mississippi.......	March 30, 1861..	78 to 7
South Carolina.....	April 3, 1861....	149 to 29
Florida...........	April 23, 1861...	Unanimously.
Arkansas.........	May 6, 1861......	Unanimously.

Among the first objects which claimed the earnest solicitude of the secession leaders in South Carolina were the enlistment of all the slaveholding States in their behalf, and non-reinforcement of the forts in Charleston harbor. Their object in obtaining possession of these strongholds was to bid defiance to the Federal authorities at

Washington, and thus not merely evade the payment of national duties on imported goods and manufactures, but also to secure the acknowledgment and sympathy of the great European powers. Their arguments and reasons upon these points were expressed in the following terms by the leading organ of secession in Charleston—the *Mercury*: "The reinforcement of the forts at this time, and under present circumstances, means coercion — war! When the forts are demanded, and refused to be delivered up to those in whom is vested the title of eminent domain, and for whose protection and defense alone they were ceded and built up; and when, the Federal Government showing a hostile purpose, it shall become proper for us to obtain possession, then it will be right for the world and Black Republicanism to expect that the State, by her authorities, will move in the premises. The people will obey the call for war, and take the forts." This expression of opinion and intention was followed by the proclamation of Gov. Pickens (two days after, Dec. 24), declaring South Carolina a separate, sovereign, free and independent State, with the right to levy war, conclude peace, negotiate treaties, leagues, covenants, and to do all acts whatever that rightly appertain to a free and independent State. Prior to this, a company of eighty men from Savannah, Ga., arrived at Charleston, and tendered their services to Gov. Pickens, under the name of "Minute Men," or "Sons of the South." No sooner had Governor Pickens' proclamation became known, than Major Anderson, who had charge of the Charleston forts, set about improving his position and strengthening his defences against the bold and traitorous designs just quoted from the Charleston *Mercury*. Up to this time Major Anderson was quite a favorite with the Charlestonians, and, if anything, was supposed to favor Southern proclivities. Subsequent events showed that he was an officer of another stamp—that, with devoted loyalty to the Union, he added military strategy and tact of no mean order, and that all his best energies, as commander of the Charleston forts, would be employed to preserve and maintain untarnished the dignity and honor of the American flag. Knowing that his then position — Fort Moultrie—was not by any means desirable or secure, in the event of any outbreak upon the part of the Secessionists, he made up his mind to remove to Fort Sumter—a place of much greater strength, and in a position better calculated to command the harbor and city of Charleston. No time was lost in carrying out the design, with a dispatch and a secrecy which all naval and military authorities pronounce admirable in the extreme. Fort Moultrie was evacuated on the night of December 26, 1860. Previous to the evacuation, the guns were spiked and the carriages destroyed by fire. The evacuation commenced a little after sun-down. The men were ordered to hold themselves in readiness, with knapsacks packed, at a moment's notice. They were reviewed on parade, and afterwards ordered to two schooners lying in the vicinity, taking with them all the necessary stores and requisites in their evacuation. Several trips were made during the night, and a great part of the provisions and camp furniture were transported under cover of night. The lightness of the moon, however, afforded but slight concealment to their movements; and in one of their trips, Lieut. Davis in command, a schooner full of soldiers and baggage passed directly under the guard-boat " Nina." Singular as it may appear, the officer of this portion of South Carolina executive authority did not take any notice of the affair. The evacuation was complete in every respect, and when fully known, took the confiding citizens of Charleston by complete surprise, and much indignation. This opinion is demonstrated beyond any cavil or doubt from the statements which appeared in the Charleston papers on the morning following the evacuation—December 27. One of them writes : " The heavy guns upon the ramparts of the fort were thrown down from their carriages and spiked; every ounce of powder and every cartridge had been removed from the magazines; and, in fact, everything like small arms, clothing, provisions, accoutrements, and other

munitions of war had been removed off and deposited—nothing but heavy ball and useless cannon remained." Another paper, in a spirit of desperate frenzy, told its readers : " Fort Moultrie, in a mutilated state, with useless guns, and flames rising in different portions of it, will stand to show the cowardly conduct of the officers who had charge of it. and who, in times of peace, basely deserted their post, and attempted to destroy a fortification which is surrounded with so many historical reminiscences, that the arm of the base scoundrel who would have ruined it should have dropped from its socket." This wise and precautionary act of Major Anderson was performed without the knowledge or concurrence of the executive authorities at Washington ; and when the fact became known to the Charlestonians, their anger was without bounds, and their threats of revenge more like the ravings of irritated maniacs than the expressions of a dissatisfied people. It was not in threats, however, that they showed that they would no longer be subject to the United States. The authorities created under the ordinance of secession appointed three commissioners to proceed to Washington, for the purpose of treating with the Government of the United States for the delivery of the forts, magazines, light-houses, and other real estate, with their appurtenances, in the limits of South Carolina, and also for an apportionment of the public debt, and for a division of all other property held by the Government of the United States as agent of the Confederated States, of which South Carolina was recently a member, and generally to negotiate as to all other measures and arrangements proper to be made and adopted in the existing relation of the parties, and for the continuance of peace and amity between this commonwealth and the government at Washington. In laying before Mr. Buchanan, the then President of the United States, this programme of their authority and power, the dismantling of Fort Moultrie and the occupancy of Fort Sumter was alluded to and commented upon, and an urgent appeal made to him to withdraw the Federal troops from Charleston, inasmuch as under the circumstances of that hour, they were nothing less than a standing menace. The arrival of the Charleston Commissioners, and their introductory correspondence with the President of the United States, was not less annoying and perplexing to His Excellency than the fact that his Secretary of War was in league with the Southern Commissioners, and that on the very day they first addressed Mr. Buchanan upon the purport of their mission to the National Capital, he, upon the plea of the violation of solemn pledges regarding the troops at Charleston, and the occupation of the forts at that city, tendered his resignation, as he could no longer hold his position as Secretary of War with honor, subjected as he was to a violation of solemn pledges and plighted faith. Mr. Buchanan at once accepted the resignation, and was thus relieved of a colleague in the administration of the United States government who had at once proved himself to be a traitor to his country and a tool in the hands of its enemies. With the Commissioners themselves Mr. Buchanan had a much more difficult game to play. It has been already shown that the main features of his Presidency were pro-slavery. Hence arose the difficulty of holding intercourse with the representatives of what he, as Chief Magistrate of the United States, was bound to consider a treasonable movement. Two of his Secretaries of State, Howell Cobb, of Georgia, and John B. Floyd, of Virginia—the former being chief of the Treasury Department, and the latter the head of the Army Bureau—had forsaken him. They knew his sentiments, and had no doubt extorted from him promises to aid the Southern cause, which, if made known, would in after years damage his character as a statesman, and deeply tarnish his reputation for political morality, honor and honesty. Such was the circumstances by which he was surrounded when compelled to enter into a correspondence with the Commissioners from South Carolina. It was clear that he could not recognize the Commissioners in an official capacity. He therefore told them so. Not desiring to be curt or to appear offensive,

Mr. Buchanan then entered into an argument, setting forth opinions expressed in his last inaugural, respecting the forts at Charleston, and said that when he learned that Major Anderson had left Fort Moultrie and proceeded to Fort Sumter, his first promptings were to command him to return to his former position, and there to await the contingencies presented in his instructions*. The events which subsequently took place at Charleston—seizure by force of two of the Federal forts, and the covering of them with the palmetto flag, instead of that of the United States; the seizure of the national custom-house and post-office, and the resignation on the same day of every officer of the Customs — Collector, Naval Officer, Surveyor, and Appraiser— had so altered the position of affairs, that Mr. Buchanan was compelled to tell the

* The following is a copy of the "Verbal Instructions to Major Anderson, First Artillery, commanding Fort Moultrie, S. C."

"You are aware of the great anxiety of the Secretary of War that a collision of the troops with the people of this State shall be avoided, and of his studied determination to pursue a course with reference to the military force and forts of this harbor, which shall guard against such a collision. He has, therefore, carefully abstained from increasing the force at this point, or taking any measures which might add to the present excited state of the public mind, or which would throw any doubt on the confidence he feels that South Carolina will not attempt by violence to obtain possession of the public works, or interfere with their occupancy.

"But as the counsel and acts of rash and impulsive persons may possibly disappoint these expectations of the Government, he deems it proper that you should be prepared with instructions to meet so unhappy a contingency. He has, therefore, directed me, verbally, to give you such instructions.

"You are carefully to avoid every act which would needlessly tend to provoke aggression, and for that reason you are not, without necessity, to take up any position which could be construed into the assumption of a hostile attitude; but *you are to hold possession of the forts in the harbor, and if attacked, you are to defend yourself to the last extremity.* The smallness of your force will not permit you, perhaps, to occupy more than one of the three forts, but an attack on, or attempt to take possession of either of them, will be regarded as an act of hostility, and you may then put your command into either of them which you may deem most proper to increase its power of resistance. *You are also authorized to take similar steps whenever you have tangible evidence of a design to proceed to a hostile act.*
                                    " D. P. BUTLER,
                     "Assistant Adjutant-General."
FORT MOULTRIE, S. C., Dec. 11, 1860.

"This is in conformity to my instructions to Major Buell.   JOHN B. FLOYD,
                                " Secretary of War."

Commissioners that it was his duty "to defend Fort Sumter as a portion of the public
property of the United States against hostile attacks, from whatever quarter they
may come, by such means as he possessed,
nor did he perceive how such a defence
could be construed into a menace against
the city of Charleston." As so much stress
was laid upon the act of Major Anderson in
dismantling Fort Moultrie and removing to
Fort Sumter, our readers will pardon us for
digressing for a few moments so as to lay
before them a brief memoir of this talented
soldier and truly patriotic citizen.

Returning to President Buchanan and
the South Carolina Commissioners, we find
the latter replying to the first of the former, under date of January 1, 1861. In this
document they set out with stating " that
South Carolina having, in the exercise of
that great right of-self government, which
underlies great political organizations, declared herself sovereign and independent,
we, as her representatives, felt no special
solicitude as to the character in which you
might recognise us." After charging Mr.
Buchanan with misquoting and miscon-
ceiving the tenor of their first communica-
tion, they proceed to meet the chief points
of his argument In doing so, they do not
fail to tarnish Mr. Buchanan's reputation
as a diplomatist and a statesman, and ar-
gue, with much apparent success, against
the inconsistency and shuffling proclivities
so strongly manifested by him in his reply
regarding the movements of Major Anderson. Indeed, so emphatic were the
opinions expressed by the Commissioners,
that Mr. Buchanan endorsed it with the
following words : " This paper, just presented to the President, is of such a character that he declines to receive it." A
considerable portion of the community felt
that Mr. Buchananan erred in the first instance by holding *any* intercourse with the
Charleston Commissioners. He was, no
doubt, anxious to postpone the threatened
rupture as long as possible, and thereby
hand to his successor, Mr. Lincoln, as a
legacy, the settlement of the great contest
which the Southern Commissioners alleged was the result of his own course of ac-

tion. That he attained his object cannot
be denied, and that promptitude and vigor
at the outset with the secestionists would
have nipped their designs in the bud is
equally incontrovertible.

The Charleston Commissioners, finding
they could do nothing with Mr. Buchanan,
returned home. Just about this time,
General Wool came out with some letters,
which, at one time, led to the hope that he
would be employed in restoring peace, if
not by the milder course of persuasion and
reason, at the point of the sword. On the
31st of December, 1860, writing to a friend
in Washington, he remarks : " Although
she"—South Carolina—" may have seized
the revenue cutter, raised her palmetto
flag over the United States' arsenal, the
Custom House, Post Office, Castle Pinckney, and Fort Moultrie, she is not out of
the United States, nor beyond the pale of
the Union. Before she can get out of their
jurisdiction or control, a reconstruction of
the Constitution must be had, *or civil war en-
sue.*" Again, in a letter written about
three weeks previous to this, Gen. Wool
wrote to General Cass, urging upon the
Cabinet at Washington to adopt such
means to save the forts at Charleston from
falling into the hands of the secessionists.
He patriotically tells General Cass that, if
he could aid the President to preserve the
Union, he hoped he would command his
services, and adds : " It will never do for
him or you to leave Washington without
every star in this Union in its place."
General Wool's opinion was disregarded, the Charleston forts were not retained,
and one by one did the slaveholding States
repudiate the authority and control of the
Federal Government ; and by the time
Mr. Buchanan took leave of the White
House, no less than six of the Southern
States had marched out of the Union.

South Carolina having taken the initia-
tive in the secession movement, her convention passed an ordinance to define and
punish treason. It provides that, in addition to that already declared treason by
the General Assembly, treason shall con-
sist only levying war against the State,
adhering to its enemies, and giving them

aid and comfort. The penalty is death, without the benefit of clergy. In this position of affairs did the year 1861 open upon what had previously been the greatest and most glorious of all democratic forms of government. Mr. Buchanan had now only two months more to complete his Presidential term. One would, therefore, have imagined that he would, in the course of even that short period, have taken some steps to retrieve the errors of the past, and preserve the public property of the United States from being plundered by what had now assumed all the characteristics of a band of rebels. Immediately after Major Anderson had removed to Fort Sumter, his communications with the City of Charleston were cut off, and shortly after the fort was closely beseiged, and extensive preparations were set on foot to capture it at all hazards. Justly, indeed, does Count Agénor De Saspin in his able book, "The Uprising of a Great People," remark :

"The Carolinians thought that they might be excused for being a little less prudent than the first magistrate of the United States. Since, moreover, they saw their pretensions sanctioned by him, why not attack the Confederation while it had a Chief who was determined to make as little defence as possible ? The weakness of Mr. Buchanan justified the confidence of Carolina. He refrained to place in the Federal fortresses troops destined to protect them against an expected assault, when a brave man, Major Anderson, took measures to defend the post that had been confided him. This unexpected resistance by which the programme was deranged, appeared as ill-timed to Mr. Buchanan as insolent to the people of Charleston, and the dispatch addressed to their Commissioners exculpates him from the crime of having sent the reinforcements, and makes excuses in pitiful terms for the conduct of Major Anderson, whom they ought to hear before condemning. In fact, Anderson acted on his own responsibility, and incurred the blame of the Minister of War, who advised in full council the surrender of the forts. The American government is as

timid as the seceded States are resolute. Our generation, which has witnessed sad spectacles, has never yet, perhaps, contemplated any more humiliating ministers— one of whom, hardly out of the Cabinet, has gone to preside over the secession convention at Montgomery, and another of whom has taken care to pave the way in advance for the revolt of the South, and to secure for it the resources of money, arms, and munitions, which it was about to need ; ministers who vote openly for the insurgents, whose financial intrigues have been proved by investigation, and whose electoral manœuvres, duplicated by embezzlement of public money, have ended in a sort of political treason, disavowed only by General Cass ; a Cabinet to continue its former course by killing with its veto the bill adopted by the legislature of Nebraska to prohibit slavery in its territory—a government falling apart by piecemeal for fear of compromising itself by resisting some part of the South ; do you know anything more shameful ? Mr. Buchanan will end as he began : for four years he has been struggling to obtain an extension of slavery ; for a month he has been favoring the plans of separation by opposing his force of inertia to the growing indignation of the North."

It was somewhere about this juncture that reports were circulated in Washington that armed bands were organizing to take possession of the Capital before the votes for President and Vice-President were counted. The then executive was somewhat alarmed at the rumors, and General Scott was authorized to make arrangements to put down the mob, should such an expedient to stifle the solemnly recorded will of the people be resorted to. While the Northern States were disagreeably influenced by such tales as the foregoing, those of the South were busily arranging their departure from the Union. The Alabama State Convention organized at Montgomery. Mississippi sent her delegates to Jacksonville, both of which passed ordinances of secession without delay. After these followed Georgia, and then Louisiana, Texas, and Florida. The attitude of the secessionists became more bold and defiant every day. Their strength was augmented, and the serious character of the crisis more and more apparent. To expel the North from the South, both in a commercial and governmental point of view, was the watchword. And it must be admitted that the sentiment was taken up with enthusiastic determination and willingness by all classes, both young and old, rich and poor, which clearly demonstrated that, come what may, the contest could not, would not be settled without a fight. To demonstrate the designs of the secessionists, it is only requisite to point to the fact that armed bodies of Florida and Alabama troops appeared before the gates of the Navy Yard of Pensacola, demanded possession, and were unresisted. They also captured Fort Barrancas. This move, it was alleged, took place in consequence of the United States government garrisoning Fort Pickens, which had previously been occupied. Property to the amount of one hundred and fifty-six thousand dollars was captured at the Pensacola Navy Yard. In addition to these, the mint at New Orleans was seized by the secessionists, and all the public property belonging to the United States was taken possession of, and whatever was useful or valuable appropriated to Southern purposes. Notwithstanding all this, the then Administration exhibited an amount of indifference to what was going on, which, to any other country in the universe, would have been totally inexplicable. The first symptoms of the intentions of the executive of South Carolina were manifested on the 9th of January, 1861. The "Star of the West," arrived off Charleston Harbor on that morning, having on board two hundred and fifty artillerymen and marines, stores, ammunition, &c. She was signalled by a steamer on the watch at the mouth of the harbor. After the usual preliminary warning by the firing of a shot across the bay, the "Star of the West" proceeded on towards Fort Sumter, bearing aloft the stars and stripes. This was the signal to fire into her from Morris Island Battery and from Fort Moultrie.

The captain deemed prudence the better part of valor, and again put to sea. Meanwhile, Major Anderson made the appearance of preparing for action by running out guns at Fort Sumter None were, however, fired ; and the first effort to reinforce the troops under the command of Major Anderson proved abortive. This affair was the preliminary act of all the difficulties which afterwards occurred.— The commander of Fort Sumter opened a sort of semi-diplomatic correspondence with Gov. Pickens, of Charleston. He sent a flag of truce with a note couched in the following terms : " Two of your batteries fired this morning on an unarmed vessel bearing the flag of my government. As I have not been notified that war has been declared by South Carolina against the United States, I cannot but think this a hostile act committed without your sanction and authority. Under this hope, I refrain from opening a fire on your batteries. I have therefore respectfully to ask whether the above-mentioned act—one which I believe without a parallel in the history of our country, or any other civilized government—was committed in obedience to your instructions ; and notify you, if it is not disclaimed, that I regard it as an act of war, and I shall not, after reasonable time for the return of my messenger, permit any vessel to pass within range of the guns of my fort. In order to save, as far as it is in my power, the shedding of blood, 1 beg you will take due notification of my decision, for t..e good of all concerned." Gov. Pickens was not to be intimidated by the threats of the hero of Fort Sumter. Accordingly, after stating the position of South Carolina towards the government at Washington, he observes that any attempt to send United States troops into Charleston Harbor would be regarded as an act of hostility—furthermore, that any attempt to reinforce Fort Sumter, or retake and resume possession of the forts within the waters of South Carolina, which Major Anderson abandoned, after spiking the cannon and doing other damage, could not but be regarded by the authorities of the State as indicative of any other purpose than the coercion of the State by the armed force of the government. After stating that special agents had been off the bar to warn approaching vessels, armed and unarmed, having troops on board to reinforce Fort Sumter, not to enter the harbor, Gov. Pickens adds: "Special orders have been given the commanders at the forts not to fire on such vessels until a shot across the bows should warn them of the prohibition of the State. Under these circumstances, the Star of the West, it is understood, this morning attempted to enter the harbor with troops, after having been notified she could not enter, and consequently she was fired into. This act is perfectly justified by me." With regard to Major Anderson's threat, Gov. Pickens was both laconic and pithy. He said: "In regard to your threat about vessels in the harbor, it is only necessary for me to say, you must be the judge of your responsibility. Your position in the harbor has been tolerated by the authorities of the State; and while the act of which you complain is in perfect consistency with the rights and duties of the State, it is not perceived how far the conduct you propose to adopt can find a parallel in the history of any country, or be reconciled with any purpose than that of your government imposing on the State the condition of a conquered province." The tenor of this reply induced Major Anderson to alter his proposed plan of operations, for he immediately acquainted Gov. Pickens that he had deemed it proper to refer the whole matter to his government, and asked for facilities for the departure and return of his messenger, Lieut. Talbot, to and from Washington. Thus, for a time, the affair was allowed to rest. Secessionism, however, was gaining ground. On the 11th of January, the Alabama Convention met at Montgomery, and passed their secession ordinance. No sooner was the news known at Mobile than the people became frantic with joy, and both day and night were spent in rejoicings of the most boisterous character. In short, to adopt the words of a Mobile paper of January 12: "The occasion seemed several Fourth of Julys, and a number of New Year's eves, va-

rious Christmases, and a sprinkling of holidays all rolled into one event. While we write, at a late hour, some enthusiastic orator is harranguing a shouting multitude from the steps of the custom-house, and all the juvenile fireworks of China and the other Indies seem to be on a grand burst of combined explosion, startling the ear with their mimic artillery of gratulation." The rejoicings were no doubt stimulated by the fact that Florida had also passed an ordinance of Secession.

In the state of affairs just described, Northern statesmen began to feel uneasy about the Union. The Legislature of the State of New York, after noting the conduct of South Carolina, already described, and the seizure of the forts and property of the United States Government in Georgia, Alabama, Louisiana, etc., resolved: "That the Legislature of New York is profoundly impressed with the value of the Union, and determined to preserve it unimpaired; that it greets with joy the recent firm, dignified and patriotic message of the President of the United States, and that we tender him, through the chief magistrate of our own State, whatever aid in men and money may be required to enable him to enforce the laws and uphold the authority of the Federal Government, and that in the defence of the Union, which has conferred prosperity and happiness upon the American people, renewing the pledge given and redeemed by our fathers, we are ready to devote our fortunes and our sacred honor." Copies of this resolution were forwarded "to the President of the Nation, and to the Governors of all the States of the Union." That it did not allay secession feeling does not require proof. In fact, such was the determination of the South to be their own rulers, that it was impossible to stem the tide of revolution which had set in.

Mr. Jefferson Davis played a most conspicuous part in the Secession game; and as his State had cast off allegiance to the Union, he appeared in the United States Senate, on the 21st of January, to take his leave of that body and justify the course of action which Mississippi had determined to pursue. Among other things, he said: "It is known to Senators who have served here that I have for many years advocated, as an essential attribute of State sovereignty, the right of a State to secede from the Union. If, therefore, I had not believed there was justifiable cause—if I had thought the State was acting without sufficient provocation—still, under my theory of government, I should have felt bound by her action. I, however, may say I think she had justifiable cause, and I approve of her acts. I confered with the people before that act was taken, and counselled them that if they could not remain, that they should take the act. I hope none will confound this expression of opinion with the advocacy of the right of a State to remain in the Union and disregard its constitutional obligations by nullification. Nullification and secession are indeed antagonistic principles. Nullification is the remedy which is to be sought and applied, within the Union, against an agent of the United States, when the agent has violated constitutional obligations, and the State assumes for itself, and appeals to other States to support it. But when the States themselves, and the people of the States, have so acted as to convince us that they will not regard our constitutional rights—then, and then for the first time, arises the question of secession in its practical application. That great man who now reposes with his fathers, who has been so often arraigned for want of fealty to the Union, advocated the doctrine of nullification, because it preserved the Union. It was because of his deep-seated attachment to the Union that Mr. Calhoun advocated the doctrine of nullification, which he claimed would give peace within the limits of the Union, and not disturb it, and only be the means of bringing the agent before the proper tribunal of the States for judgment. Secession belongs to a different class of rights, and is to be justified upon the basis that the States are sovereign. The time has been, and I hope the time will come again, when a better appreciation of our Union will prevent any one denying that each State is a sovereign in its own right. Therefore, I say I concur in the act of my State, and feel bound by it. It is by this confounding of nullification and secession that the name of another great man has been invoked to justify the coercion of a seceding State. The phrase "to execute the law," as used by General Jackson, was applied to a State refusing to obey the laws and still remaining in the Union. I remember well when Massachusetts was arraigned before the Senate. The record of that occasion will show that I said, if Massachusetts, in pursuing the line of steps, takes the last step which separates her from the Union, the right is hers, and I will neither vote one dollar nor one man to coerce her, but I will say to her, 'God speed!'" Mr. Davis argued that the equality spoken of in the Declaration of Independence was the equality of a class in political rights, referring to the charge against George III. for inciting insurrection, as proof that it had no reference to slaves. "But we have proclaimed our independence. This is done with no hostility or any desire to injure any section of the country, nor even for our pecuniary benefit, but from the high and solid foundation of defending and protecting the rights we inherited, and transmitting them unshorn to our posterity. There will be peace if you so will it, and you may bring disaster on every part of the country, if you thus will have it. And if you will have it thus, we will invoke the God of our fathers, who delivered them from the paw of the lion, to protect us from the ravages of the bear; and thus putting our trust in God, and our own firm hearts and strong arms, we will vindicate and defend the rights we claim."

Such were the language and sentiments used by the present head of the Southern Confederacy. They clearly indicated a determined and firm purpose, not merely upon his part, but the slaveholding States generally, to struggle for and obtain a separation from the Union. It has been shown that the example set by South Carolina had no small effect in precipitating the contest, which any politician of foresight regarded as inevitable. The first step towards forming a separate and independent government of the secessionists was inaugurated by the meeting of a congress of delegates from all the States which had seceded. This took place at Montgomery, Alabama; and on the 8th of February it unanimously agreed to a constitution and provisional government, which were ordered to go into immediate operation. The idea of compromise or re-construction of the Federal Constitution was never once mooted; indeed, from the tone and temper of this assembly, the bare mention of such a proposition would have been squelched at the outset, and discussion upon it put down, inasmuch as the president of the congress was Howell Cobb, of Georgia, one of Mr. Buchanan's ministry, and who, in that capacity, did his best to bring about the disruption which has taken place between the North and the South. Having agreed to a constitution and a government, the next step was to elect a President and Vice-President. This was done with singular alacrity, and the choice fell upon Jefferson Davis and Alexander H. Stephens. Mr. Davis lost no time in selecting the members of his Cabinet. On the 21st of February, he nominated Mr. Toombs as Secretary of State, Mr. Memminger Secretary of the Treasury, and Mr. L. Pope Walker Secretary of War. The Confederate Congress confirmed the nomination, and these gentlemen at once entered upon their official duties. As Mr. Toombs was the first prime minister of the Southern Confederacy, it will not be out of place to quote his message to the people of Georgia, telegraphed from Washington on the 23d of December:

"I came here to secure your constitutional rights, and to demonstrate to you that you can get no guarantee for those rights from your Nothern confederates. The whole subject was referred to a Committee of Thirteen in the Senate. I was appointed on the Committee, and accepted the trust. I submitted propositions, which, so far from receiving decided support from a single member of the Republican party of the Committee, were all treated with derision or contempt. A vote was then taken in the Committee on amendments to the Constitution proposed by Hon. J. J. Crittenden, and each and all of them were voted against unanimously by the Black Republican members of the Committee. In addition to these facts, a majority of the Black Republican members of the Committee declared distinctly that they had no guarantees to offer, which was silently acquiesced in by the other members. The Black Republican members of this Committee of Thirteen are representative men of the party and section, and, to the extent of my information, truly represent them.

"The Committee of Thirty-three on Friday adjourned for a week, without coming to any vote, after solemnly pledging themselves to vote on all the propositions then before them on that day. It is controlled by the Black Republicans, your enemies, who only seek to amuse you with delusive hope until your election, that you may defeat the friends of secession. If you are deceived by them, it shall not be my fault. I have put the test fairly and frankly. It is decisive against you now. I tell you, upon the faith of a true man, that all further looking to the North for security for your constitutional rights in the Union ought to be instantly abandoned. It is fraught with nothing but ruin to yourselves and your posterity. Secession by the 4th day of March next should be thundered from the ballot-box by the unanimous vote of Georgia on the 2d day of January next. Such a voice will be your best guarantee for liberty, security, tranquility, and glory.   R. TOOMBS."

While all these unmistakable symptoms of separation was going forward, there were Union-loving parties who held the hope of being able to avert the threatened calamities of civil war. Accordingly, a body, terming itself the Peace Convention, met at Washington, and organized permanently — ex-President Tyler being called to the chair. Having been in session from the 5th to the 27th of February, they drew up a report of their deliberations, and submitted to the Senate of the United States a plan of adjustment which included seven amendments to the Constitution of the United States. We have transcribed these amendments, showing, as they do, the length which Union-loving men were disposed to go in order to avert anarchy, bloodshed, and confusion :

"SEC. 1. In all the present territory of the United States north of the parallel of 36 deg. 30 min. of north latitude, involuntary servitude, except in punishment of crime, is prohibited. In all the present territory south of that line, the *status* of persons held to involuntary service or labor, as it now exists, shall not be changed : nor shall any law be passed by Congress or the Territorial Legislature to hinder or prevent the taking of such persons from any of the States of this Union to said territory, nor to impair the right arising from said relation ; but the same shall be subject to judicial cognizance in the Federal courts, according to the course of the common law. When any Territory north or south of said line, within such boundary as Congress may prescribe, shall contain a population equal to that required for a member of Congress, it shall, if its form of Government be republican, be admitted into the Union on an equal footing with the original States, with or without involuntary servitude, as the constitution of such State may provide.

"SEC. 2. No territory shall be acquired by the United States, except by discovery, and for naval and commercial stations, depots, and transit routes, without the concurrence of a majority of all the Senators from States which allow involuntary servitude, and a majority of all the Senators from States which prohibit that relation : nor shall territory be acquired by treaty, unless the votes of a majority of the Senators from each class of States hereinbefore mentioned be cast as a part of the two-thirds majority necessary to the ratification of such treaty.

"SEC. 3. Neither the constitution nor any amendment thereof shall be construed to give Congress power to regulate, abolish or control within any State the relation established or recognized by the laws thereof touching persons held to labor or involuntary service therein, nor to interfere with or abolish involuntary service in the District of Columbia without the consent of Maryland, and with-

out the consent of the owners, or making the owners who do not consent just compensation ; nor the power to interfere with or prohibit representatives and others from bringing with them to the District of Columbia, retaining, and taking away, persons so held to labor or service ; nor the power to interfere with or abolish involuntary service in places under the exclusive jurisdiction of the United States, within those States and Territories where the same is established or recognized ; nor the power to prohibit the removal or transportation of persons held to labor or involuntary service in any State or Territory of the United States to any other State or Territory thereof, where it is established or recognized by law or usage ; and the right during transportation, by sea or river, of touching at ports, shores, and landings, and of landing in case of distress, shall exist ; but not the right of transit in or through any State or Territory, or of sale or traffic, against the laws thereof. Nor shall Congress have power to authorize any higher rate of taxation on persons held to labor or service than on land. The bringing into the District of Columbia of persons held to labor or service, for sale, or placing them in depots to be afterwards transferred to other places for sale as merchandise, is prohibited.

"SEC. 4. The third paragraph of the second section of the fourth article of the constitution shall not be construed to prevent any of the States, by appropriate legislation, and through the action of their judicial and ministerial officers, from enforcing the delivery of fugitives from labor to the person to whom such service or labor is due.

"SEC. 5. The foreign slave trade is hereby forever prohibited ; and it shall be the duty of Congress to pass laws to prevent the importation of slaves, coolies, or persons held to service or labor, into the United States and Territories from places beyond the limits thereof.

"SEC. 6. The first, third, and fifth sections, together with this section, of these amendments, and the third paragraph of the second section of the first article of the constitution, and the third paragraph of the second section of the fourth article thereof, shall not be

The Roll of the Union Army.

THE SEVENTH REGIMENT OF THE N. Y. S. M.

In entering upon this portion of our task, we select the Seventh Regiment, of New York, as the first which merits record in these pages. It was the first to leave the city for the purpose of protecting the National Capital from the intended invasion of the Secessionists.

With a promptitude which merits all commendation, the men composing the Seventh Regiment mustered for their march after only a few hours' notice. This was at the time of the great uprising of the people of the Northern States, when the cry was general, loud, and determined for an appeal to arms. The beating of drums and the sound of martial music, the waving of flags, and the exhibition of Union badges, cockades, breastpins, brooches, charms, etc., upon the person of every man, woman or child who ventured forth, whether in the pursuit of business or pleasure, was the order of the day. The dull, heavy tramp of the military was heard, and the glittering of their burnished arms seen in almost all our thoroughfares. The keen, shrill blast of the bugle's morning-call, and the measured tread of sentinels around the recruiting depots, told unmistakably that the country was at war—that its peace had been broken and its time-honored Constitution placed in jeopardy. Then, too, could be heard the warning voice of patriotic statesmen, the solemn prayers of gospel ministers, and the no less fervent and sincere ejaculations of "Amen!" from their hearers. The wild hurrahs with which every sentiment breathing loyalty and devotion to the Union was taken up, and the avidity with which fathers delivered their sons to the requirements of their country, and wives consented that their husbands should forsake them for a time and venture upon the battle-field — that arena of deadly conflict, carnage and human slaughter—was no less marvelous than it was commendable. Patriotism so noble, so pure, so self-denying, seemed almost an inspiration of Heaven. No matter what country or what people we call to mind, the conduct and bearing of the citizens of the Northern States was one continued round of enthusiasm and genuine patriotism — which, if at all equalled, has never been surpassed.

It was in this state of things that the Seventh Regiment, of New York, was called upon to repair, without delay, to Washington, which was then threatened with an attack by the rebels. It had been preceded by the Sixth (Massachusetts) a day or two before, and, in passing through Baltimore, had a narrow escape from the "Blood Tubs" and "Plug Uglies" who have ever disgraced the chief city of Maryland. The character of the attack and its results will be noticed when we give the muster-roll of the Massachusetts regiment.

The news of the attack at Baltimore had been made known while the Seventh Regiment was being mustered for the march. They expected to pass through Baltimore; and, from the threats of the Secessionists, it was considered there would be bloody work. Nevertheless, although impressed with a full conviction of the dangers which threatened them, they were nothing daunted—they felt that they were on the side of justice and truth; and, with a firm reliance that the God of Battles would protect them from the murderous intentions of their enemies, they set out from New York on the afternoon of Friday, the 19th of April.

The Seventh Regiment has ever been one of the most popular belonging to the city of New York—consequently, it was to be expected that they would receive a great ovation. Nor were those who indulged in such anticipations disappointed. The decorations of the streets along the line of march were superb. The thousands and tens of thousands who congregated along Broadway rent the air with cheers and plaudits of the most deafening and enthusiastic kind. Complimentary and highly gratifying as was the reception which was bestowed upon the Seventh Regiment on its departure, the men composing it were not much, if at all, elated at the honors which their fellow-citizens showered upon them. It was easy to trace in the solemn countenance of each and every man that he was setting out upon an important mission. They were men who evidently felt that to them was assigned the duty of protecting with jealous care the Stars and Stripes which were emblazoned on their regimental standards. To the credit of every man, from the colonel down to the humblest private, the march was conducted with order, precision and strict military discipline. Although much temptation existed, there was not the slightest symptoms of a too free indulgence in "stimulants"—a circumstance which shows how careful Colonel Lefferts and his officers must have been.

In connection with the march down Broadway an incident occurred which is worth mention. On the balcony of the store of Ball, Black & Co., Col. Anderson took up a position, that he might have a full view of the magnificent appearance of the regiment. When he was discovered, there was a shout which the detractors of his fame ought to have heard. There stood before the masses a man who had proved that in his keeping the national standard of the United States was safe, and that they who imputed to him anything appertaining to treachery or treason were libelers and slanderers of the basest kind. Upon the occasion to which we allude, he was duly honored for his gallant conduct at Fort Sumter; and no doubt every man of the Seventh felt that that conduct was worthy of imitation, and made up his mind to "go and do likewise."

It was originally intended that the Seventh Regiment should proceed through Baltimore, and if opposed in that city, to inflict a signal chastisement upon the rowdies who so maliciously assaulted the Sixth Massachusetts Regiment that very day. They had prepared themselves for the dangerous task which they proposed to execute. In addition to their small arms, the regiment took along with them two howitzer guns, to be worked by the troop and engineer corps. The officers, too, were provided with pistols of Colt's construction. Had any engagement taken place at Baltimore, the consequences would have been fearful. Having arrived at Philadelphia, circumstances occurred which induced Col. Lefferts to change his plan of operations. He was notified by the Governor of Maryland and the civic authorities of Baltimore that the soil of Maryland should not be invaded by the march of Federal troops *en route* to Washington. This mandate would in all probability have been disregarded, had there not been a difficulty in finding railway transit, inasmuch as the superintendent of the Baltimore and Ohio Railroad positively refused to provide cars for the transport of the regiment over his road. Another course had therefore to be adopted, and an order was reluctantly issued for the men to leave the cars at Philadelphia, and pass the time as best they could until some other arrangement was made to send them forward to Washington. Here Col. Lefferts displayed the utmost consideration for his men. He telegraphed his position to the War Department at Washington, and also sent on to New York for provisions and all other necessaries, which were to be forwarded by water to Annapolis, Maryland. Whilst waiting for means of transportation, an incident of peculiar interest took place. The regiment was temporarily bouaiaced in the railroad depot; thousands of visitors thronged the building, looking at the men with the greatest possible interest, and wishing them the best success in the important duty which they had taken in hand. In the midst of the bustle and excitement which prevailed, an aged lady, of respectable appearance, entered the building, carrying a large market-basket on each arm, and anxiously desiring to see some of the officers. One of the sergeants was directed to ascertain the nature of her business, when she stated it in something like the following terms:

"I heard that some of you soldier men hadn't got anything to eat, and specially that you were out of bread. Now, I've brought you some that is real good, home-made bread—some of it I made myself, and some of it a neighbor made for me. Here, take it—you are welcome to it. I want to find some one to give it to." Some of the men, of course, proposed to pay her for it; but she positively declined, saying: "No, no; I want to give it to you. I had a boy once who was a soldier in the regular army; he was all through the Mexican war, and he was killed in battle. I always feel as if I couldn't over do too much for the soldiers. I can't give you much, boys," continued she, wiping away the tears that *would* come at the thought of her own "boy"; "but here's my bread, and I hope some of you may like it. There's a plate of nice, fresh butter there, too; and you may have the basket, and the plates, and everything. May be my boy has wanted some bread some time, and I hope some mother gave it to him." Here the old lady, after a minute's struggle, broke entirely down, and with the words—"My poor boy—my dear Alfred!"—she hurried away, leaving her baskets behind her. This incident was not without its good effect, for not one of all the spectators but was touched to the heart by the sincere grief of the poor old woman, and not one but thought better of a cause that could command a gift so earnest and pure, though so humble; and perhaps a few were made to think more tenderly of other mothers who might so soon be called to mourn other sons, slain by their country's enemies. The old lady's name was found to be Magilton, and she had one son educated at West Point, one killed in Mexico, and a third son is Magilton, the circus performer, who was one of the very cleverest men in the whole profession. This last-named one, recently, while doing the "trapeze" performance in England, fell from a height of thirty-five feet, striking on his back and shoulders, inflicting injuries of which he may probably die.

It is by no means necessary to recount all the incidents that took place during the delay of the regiment at the Baltimore and Ohio Railroad depot. The men made themselves as comfortable as possible under the circumstances. The military authorities at Washington were very inattentive to Col. Lefferts' inquiry what to do; and after a halt of fourteen hours, he determined to proceed by sea to Annapolis. He made arrangements for this purpose, and with as little loss of time as possible, he marched his men and baggage on board the steamer Boston on Saturday evening, April 20th.

The voyage was somewhat perilous, from the vast crowds of men and officers on board the Boston. Great privations and inconveniences were endured, but all bore up with the most courageous fortitude. It was 4 P. M. of the 22d before the Seventh Regiment landed at the dock of the Naval School, at Annapolis. Fresh difficulties had to be encountered at this point, added to which were the flying rumors that the enemy were in strong force along the road by which the regiment was to march to Washington. For all this, they did not evince any fear or trepidation. The general feeling was in favor of having a brush with the rebels ere they arrived at the National Capital. They felt, too, that they were bound to give the South some tangible proof that they were not so easily mastered as the Southern rebels boasted. After a series of delays, Col. Lefferts was enabled to take his departure for Washington, which it reached in safety, amid the hearty congratulations of the citizens and to the great relief of the executive authorities, who had spent several days and nights of anxiety. In all the march from New York to Washington every man of the regiment gave sufficient evidence of every soldierly quality. They bore hunger and privation of the severest kind without a murmur; nor were they less remarkable for their readiness to perform the severe military duty which was assigned them. In the trenches upon Arlington Heights, and on sentry, they have, one and all, proved efficient and trustworthy soldiers. They were the means of saving the National Capital at a very critical moment; and those who run them down for returning when their term of service had expired, not merely reason illogically, but do the men a measure of much injustice.

The Seventh Regiment was only engaged for thirty days' service; and when their time was up, the United States authorities made arrangements to allow them to return home. This did not arise from any distrust of their patriotism and loyalty, nor the least feeling of dissatisfaction with their extreme efficiency as soldiers in the field. On the contrary, all these desirable traits in the defender of his country in the hour of danger had been fully exemplified, and were officially endorsed by the highest military authorities at Washington.* It

* See supplementary note at the end of the roll.

was motives of discreet prudence and policy which swayed the Secretary of War to send home the Seventh Regiment. As it had always been a most popular regiment on the battle-field, so its departure therefrom was regarded with extreme regret. This was very plainly manifested when their farewell parade took place at Washington. Every one, civilian and military, vied with each other who could most honor a body of men who had proved themselves an ornament to the profession of arms and a lasting credit to the city from which they hailed They left Washington, on their return for New York, on Friday, the 30th of June; and before doing so, conferred an act of extreme kindness and hospitality to one of the regiments less affluent than themselves. They presented to them all their camp equipage and many other articles equally useful and valuable to a campaigning army. The recipients of this desirable gift were the New York Fire Zouaves.

On Saturday, the 1st of June, the Seventh Regiment re-entered New York, where a hearty greeting was bestowed upon them. Detractive remarks had been made by some censorious minds, who never can perceive excellence in any man or body of men, except they are themselves the centre of such excellence. It was, therefore, endeavored to make the reception as cool as possible. But the effort failed—signally failed—and Colonel Lefferts and his men entered their native city amid the loud and enthusiastic welcomes of congregated thousands, who uttered sincere and heartfelt thanks that the great disposer of all events had not thinned the ranks, either by the ravages of disease, or the more terrible havoc of bloody war. The regiment left 921 strong, and returned numbering 1255,* officers and men—another proof of the extreme care of the commander and the great attention of the medical officers, Dr. T. M. Cheeseman and Dr. John W. Dalton. It would, however, be an act of injustice if, in this brief sketch, we omitted to note that much praise is due to the chaplain of the Seventh, the Rev. Mr. Weston. The Philosopher who scans the universe—takes cognizance of the relationship of cause and effect—of man—what he is and what he can be made, according as his actions are swayed by the proper exercise of the laws planted within his triune nature: body, head and heart— is well aware that in proportion to the influence which the moral sentiments control our every-day habits, and induce sobriety, correctness of deportment and rectitude of purpose, so will be the healthy condition of all those powers which make up our physical organization, and either sharpen or blunt the most glo-

* This includes a number of volunteers who afterwards joined.

rious portion of existing humanity—intellect. Influenced by the truth of this philosophical theorem, the Rev. Chaplain of the Seventh was "instant in season and out of season." His solicitude for the moral and spiritual advancement of the troops under his ministerial charge enabled him to impart such lessons as induced, if not practical piety, correct morals. These prevented undue excess in anything dangerous to the physical constitution, preserved health, and rendered the men comfortable and happy under all the sufferings, hardships and privations which they had to encounter.

Having now glanced at the part which the New York National Guard took in the campaign against the Southern rebels, we deem it a mere act of justice to notice more in detail the slanderous imputations cast upon them in consequence of their returning home before the termination of the conflict. It has been alleged against this regiment, that owing to their return, they manifested a lack of military courage, proved that they were only milk-and-water patriots, and more fitted for *parlor* and *drawing-room* drill than to perform all or any of the fatiguing duties of a campaign-life in an enemy's country. The facts given above confute such accusations, and we feel bound to say that the spirit which actuated their authors was not becoming, and their intention and object spiteful and malevolent in the extreme.

A cursory glance at the *true* state of the case will show that the Seventh Regiment was perfectly entitled to return, whilst it will be equally clear that they proved themselves soldiers of the foremost class, and did not lack a single quality essential to an army going forth to conquer an enemy. The Seventh Regiment mustered at an hour's call. It was engaged to protect the Capital until the U. S. Government could send forward troops from all quarters of the Union. From the time when their services were called for until they set out upon the march was only twelve hours. The prompt response of Col. Lefferts and his men at once checked the designs of the rebel army, and kept back the hordes of traitorous adventurers who contemplated the capture of Washington. Now, for this one act alone they are entitled to the thanks and lasting gratitude of the country. It was a deed which foiled the enemy at the outset, and drew from him imprecations—loud and hellish.

Those who murmured at the return of the Seventh Regiment should have remembered that its members are mainly composed of men who are engaged in business pursuits. In the extreme hurry with which they were dispatched, the greater portion of them left their affairs in a very disarranged condition, and for them to have remained longer away would have been totally ruinous to their interests and property. It should be borne in mind that their period of service was thirty days; and at the end of that time, such was the excellent state of the Union army, that there was no pressing necessity for their services; consequently, every one must admit that it would have been both ungenerous and unjust to ask them to remain any longer at military duties, and thereby cause their business affairs to get into greater confusion and probably irreparable arrangement. Upon a calm and unbiased retrospect of the conduct of this regiment, from the time it set out, on the 19th of April, until its return, on the 1st of June, all reasonable-minded men will admit that it has been equal to any other body of troops in the field, that both officers and men performed every duty assigned them in a commendable and efficient manner, and that they bore an amount of fatigue and privation which would test the physical powers and severely try the nerves of the hardiest veteran campaigner. It is ever the part of the envious to carp and cavil at everything and everybody superior to themselves—and, as regards the Seventh Regiment, this is particularly so—showing how apt and striking are the words of the poet:

" —————— Base envy withers
   At another's joy, and hates the excellence
   It cannot reach."

Muster Roll of the Seventh Regiment, N. Y. S. M.

REGIMENTAL STAFF.

Colonel, - - - - Marshall Lefferts.
Lt. Colonel, - Wm. A. Pond, did not go.
Major, - - - - Alexander Shaler.
Adjutant, - - - - J. Henry Liebenau.
Quartermaster, - - L. W. Winchester.
Commissary, - - - - Wm. Patten.
Paymaster, - - - - A. Kemp.
As-'t Paymaster, - - Meredith Howland.
Chaplain, - - - - Roswell H. Weston.
Ordinance Officer, - - John A. Baker.
Surgeon, - - - - - Cheeseman.
1st Ass't Surgeon, - - John C. Dalton.

2nd Ass't Surgeon, - - - ——— Tuttle.
Hos. Steward, - - - - ——— Bedford.

NON-COMMISSIONED STAFF.

Sergeant Major, - - - R. C. Rathbone.
Color Sergeants, - - - S W. Scott.
"   "   - - - F. H. Pearce.
Commissary's Sergeant, L. L. S Clearman.
Act. Quart'r Sgt. - - - Isaac Dean.
"   "   "   - - - R. C Weed.
Ordinance Sgt. - - - - John H. Draper.
Right Gen l Guide, - - - S. O. Ryder.
Left Gen'l Guide, - - - J. J. Morrison.

FIRST COMPANY.

Captain, W. B. Beosel,
1st Lieut. C. H. Meday,
2nd " J. L. Hanway,
Orderly Sgt. Wm. H. Hume,
2nd " H. C. Robe,
3rd " P. G. Bogart,
4th " H. M. Funston,
5th " F. O. Pierce,
1st Corporal, J. K. Shephard,
2nd " O S. Wilson,
3rd " C. H. Ketchen,
4th " Wm. Davidson,
5th " G. M. Diggs,
6th " D. L. Hays,
7th " E. Trenor,

PRIVATES.

Allen, J. B.
Archer, A. S.
Asten, T. S.
Appeles, T. L.
Buchanan, D. D.
Brincherhoff, W. B.
Borrowson. O.
Bryce, G. W G.
Brown, W. H.
Bogart, H. Y.
Belknap, Aug.
Barr, S. O.
Briggs, C. A.
Bang, T. J.
Barnum, H. C.
Bell, S. L.
Clark, N.
Clark, J. R.
Cooper, Wm. H.
Cooper, T. W.
Cable, J. H.
Clough, Henry
Cook, G. T.
Cowperthwaite, F. H.
Derferndolf, C. P.
Davidge, R. C.
Druslow, N. J.
Davis, B. F.
Donaldson, W. J.
Darling, H.
Ellis, Henry,
Evans, R. B.
Eckel, F. H.
Forbes, Ed.

Grant, T. J.
Griffith, T. H.
Gomperts, G. S.
Hume, G. W.
Howe, C. H.
Hyde, E. J.
Hart, O H.
Hart, F. H.
Hewlett, A. C.
Hamilton, Robert
Henberer, C.
Hashlasher, George
Humphreys, N. S.
Imnea, John H.
Kingsland, D C.
Kirkland, T. S
Kahler, Frederick
Kurtz, William
Kelly, J. G;
Leggett, Samuel
Lindemann, H.
Le Fort, George
Lyon,
Lowber, J. H.
Murray, James
McIlvaine, F. E.
McKruaw J. P.
Merkle, Aug.
Meday, G. H.
Miller, J. H.
Mott, J. W.
Marguardt, C.
Orpen, C. W.
Patterson, Luke
Perry, D. O.
Plass,
Rogers, G. L.
Rawson, E. B.
Reynolds, C. L.
Ring, G. W.
Spolford, C. H.
Sibell, J. W.
Slocomb, T. D.
Spellman, N. B.
Snyder, E. L.
Shields, Wm. H.
Sumner, A. C.
Slagg, H. B.
Saunders, G. F.
Simonson, J. H.
Smith, F. A.
Spring, E. A.
Swartz, J. H.

Sharp, William A.
Seaver, T A.
Stromay, Albert
Toed, R. C.
Trenor, H. H.
Trenor, J. F.
Trenor, J. J.
Trenor, J. Jr.
Thwait, S. C.
Tugman, C. A.
Villiers, Thomas
Van Ness, George
Villeplait, A. B.
Villeplait, W. D. H.
Weicker, John
Wilbur, E. R.
Wetmore, Aug.
Waldro , R. S.
Wheeler, W. P.
Whiteman,
Yost, Henry.

SECOND COMPANY.

Capt. Emmons Clark,
1st Lieut. Noah L. Farnham,
2nd Lieut. Edward Bernard,
1st Sgt. Peter Palmer,
2nd Sgt. Joseph E. Macfarland,
3rd Sgt. Charles S. Van Norden,
4th Sgt. Henry B. Dyer,
5th Sgt. David Miller,
1st Corp'l Richard F. Ware,
2nd " Richard D. Fonder,
3rd " George A. Bernard,
4th " Charles S. Janes,
Lance Cor. Rob't S. Gould, Jr.
     " Reginald H. Williams,
     " Rodney C. Ward,
     " Thos. W. K. Holder,

PRIVATES.

W. G. Allison,
R. Allison,
J. B. Amerman,
F. G. Ageus,
J. B. Ames, Jr.
H. H. Alden,
J. M. Alden,
W. T. Bucken,
R. C. Buckau,

H. Bristow,
G. S. Burnet,
B. Brower,
J. C. Bloomfield,
W. A. Burtis,
A. M. Burtis,
O. F. Booth,
D. T. Boardman,
G. L. Buckley,
E. Baker,
W. H. Codey,
S. W. Codey,
W. O. Chapman,
A. A. Curtis,
W. Colton,
A. M. Chace,
G. Debenham,
W. L. Darling,
H. P. Eveleth,
W. Edwards,
W. R. Eadie,
G. M. Evans,
W. T. Farnham,
S. Florence,
A. Findlay,
F. Foster,
A. Garrison,
H. G. Gregory,
F. Gregory,
B. Gregory,
H. Gordon,
J. F. Gittens, Jr.
H. Hives,
F. A. Harter,
J. N. Havens,
N. A. Halsey,
H. P. Halsey,
R. F. Hasfield,
A. Hatfield, Jr.
T. I. Hatfield,
O. Hall,
C. S. Hill,
W. M Haddock,
H. G. Healey,
W. Hadley,
M. L. Jones,
J. S. King,
R. H. Lane,
J. Lawrence,
R. W. Leonard,
R. McKinley,
W A. McDonald,
W. H. Mix,
E. Mix,
J. B. Mix,
S. T. Mather,
T. D. Mather,
E. McManus,
J. W. Miller,
D. J. Miller,
F. S. Morrison, Jr.
W. Nodine,
C. Overton,
J. Oakey,
H. L. Phalen,
G. Putnam,
H. M. Porter,
G. S. Phipps,
D. Postley,
W. S. Phyfe,
J. W. Powell,
G. V. Quillard,
J. F. Russell,
J. Roome,
C. J. Ruscher,
J. W. Roome,
G. W. Selover,
H. F. Savage,
R. I. Salisbury,
S. R. Struthers,
C. S. Sterling,
J. Stevenson,

C. C. Shelley,
E. W. Stratton,
W. B. See,
J. A. Smith,
G. B. Smith,
G. M. Smith,
E. Sturgis,
D. H. Tuttle,
C. H. Tay,
G. T. Tybring,
J. H. Taylor,
A. Taylor,
J. W. Vandewater,
J. S. Vanderbilt,
J. V. W. Vandervoort,
W. Van Duzer,
J. Wilson,
J. Williamson, Jr.
E. Ward,
G. J. L. Wright,
D. T. Way,
E. Williams,
E. B. Webster,
E. Whitfield.

THIRD COMPANY.

Captain, James Price,
1st Lieut. John J. Wickstead,
2nd "   George T Haws,
Sergeant, John W. Murray,
"   Theo. B. Stephens,
"   Richard L. Leggett,
"   Louis Fitzgerald,
"   Jos. Dore,
Corporal, Wm. P Baily,
"   De Witt Clinton,
"   Chas. B. Owen,
"   G. D. Tracy,
"   C. R. Crane,
"   Louis B. Rader.

PRIVATES.

Abbot, Chas. A.
Allen, Henry
Barret, John
Banks, J. E.
Bogart, Chas. C.
Burdett, J. Jr.
Bend, Wm. B.
Bacon, Geo. W.
Barnes, A. C.
Burton, W. C.
Barker, C J.
Butler, H Jr.
Broderick, Wm. E.
Beers, W. H.
Brown, Chas. L.
Bennedict, E. F.
Bunee, T. D.
Bomford, G. N.
Chapman, Jos. H.
Colgate, Clinton G.
Conroy, Thos. L.
Conroy, Wm F.
Collins, Wm. S.
Collins, Geo. S.
Cook, Vincent L.
Covell, Chas S.
Cheesman, T. M.
Clinton, C. W.
Clowes, T F.
Crane, L P.
Cheesbrough, Wm. H.
Cheesbrough, R. A.
Doolittle, Jas. K.
Eastman,
Elliot, Thos.
Ferry, Darins Jr.
Foster Clinton,

Fish, L. A.
Geodar, Thomas V.
Graham, Jos. F.
Gnlager, Philip
Hickcox, T. N.
Horst, Fred. R.
Hale, Wm. D.
Hughes, Charles
Holt, Ed. O.
Hoxie, Wm. E.
Irving, Thos. R.
Jordan. C. N.
Kennedy, Chas.
Lawrence, Geo. P.
Lewis, Curtis
Merle, Chas. F.
Mott, Henry H.
Melligan, S. G.
McKibben, G. H.
Marshall, George
Marshall, Alexander
Oakley, Alfred
Oakley, N. H.
Portington, R. C.
Peterson, C.
Pollard, D. A.
Pollock, W. J.
Platt, Wm. C.
Radcliffe, H. G.
Robinson, W. G.
Reeve, Isaac T.
Kequel, G. W.
Sebert, J. F.
Sebart, Jno.
Sexton, S. J. M.
Spooner, H. F.
Simonson, Jos.
Smith, Eugene B.
Smith, A. M. C. Jr.
Smith, W. H.
St. John, W. M.
Tuthill, S. B.
Tremain, H. E.
Tremain, W. R.
Van Riper, Jas.
Van Wyck, W. E.
Van Houten, Isaac
Vap'nuck,
Warren, James R.
Warren, Jos. C.
Wellman, W. P.
Whitney, W. M.
Woolf, H. G.
Wright, John G.
Wright, David F.
Wicks, Geo. J.
Wilson, Jas. W.
White, O. G.
Watkins, W. L.
Yard, W. S.

FOURTH COMPANY.

Captain, W. H. Riblet,
1st Lieu't, William Gurney,
2nd "   John W Bogert,
1st Sgt., Peter M. Mevers,
2nd "   Edward W. Little,
3rd "   Jeremiah V. Meserole,
4th "   Alfred B. Chapman,
5th "   Henry Everdell,
1st Corp'l, Charles E. Bogert,
2nd "   Robert H. Eddy,
3rd "   Edward R. Young,
4th "   James Farnam,
Drummer, Henry Eidman.

PRIVATES.

Aymore, J. S.
Aikman, A. H.

Bunting, R. S.
Bauvelt, J, H.
Beggs, J. W.
Breeden, Abner H.
Breeden, Charles E.
Balen, Peter Jr.
Bruor, Thomas
Burdick, C. E.
Canfield, Jesse, W.
Carter, Herman G.
Carpenter, Silas S.
Crary, Charles H.
Crist, Stephen B.
Crocker, George A.
Cheeseborough, State
Collamore, Gilman
Davenport, Charles F.
Dougherty, Horace F.
Dickerson, George A.
Dubois, J. S. L.
Ewen, Edward D.
Ewen, Austin D.
Ewen, Norman
Earle, Edward
Everdell, Francis
Edwin, W. A.
Fay, Logan
Fay, P. H.
Fairbanks, Charles M.
Ferry, Edwin W.
Fielding, W. S.
Fisk, W. E.
Farrington, Adam
Gautier, Samuel
Gaston, Wm.
Haywood, Melville
Hall, H. M.
Halsted, Robert
Harrison, Edward A.
Hennesey, John F. Jr.
Hollingshead, William M.
Holly, Henry H.
Huntington, Charles, P.
Husted, Theo. I.
Hyde, M W.
Hickox, Charles R.
Honeywell, Charles R.
Jarvis, John
Karr, Frank D.
Kipp, William H.
Lawrence, G. A.
Lawrence, Edward L.
Lambert, William
Lefferts, Marshall, Jr.
Little, John L.
Mallon, James E.
Manning, G. F.
Marshall, Alex. S
Mills, James
Miller, W. R.
Merrit, Abraham
Morse, L. W.
Moies, John E.
Nichols, William L.
Nugent, Henry
Olssen, Edward J.
Osborne, E. R.
Owen, Mortimer B.
Outcalt, Cornelius B.
Peacock, Thomas R.
Ridden, John C.
Ryan, James E.
Roome, W. H.
Sanford, George H.
Sangster, George
Smith, Samuel J.
Smith, Frank K.
Smith, William H.
Smith, Ernest L.
Smith, Milton
Snodgrass, Arch'd A.
Spaulding, Zeph. S.

Starr, Samuel H.
Steele, William S.
Steele, Peter B.
Sharp, S. C.
Sinclair, Hyatt
Swords, Charles H.
Taylor, Jos. D.
Weyman, Edward H. Jr.
Wood, William H.
Waltz, Ernst L.
Wright, W. C.
Woodhouse, L. G.

FIFTH COMPANY.

Capt. W. A. Speaight,
Lieut. C. Corley,
"   J. Gaylor,
Sgt. W T. Sprole,
"   J. D Earle,
"   J. P. Miller,
"   J. B. Holbrook,
"   W. Seward. Jr.
Corp'l E. K. Halsted,
"   D. D. Brainted,
"   W. Wall, Jr.
"   G. G. Barnes,
"   W. Scott,
"   D. C. Vanderbilt,
"   T. E. Whitney,
"   J. L. Eckel,

PRIVATES.

Baker, T. E.
Barrett, G. P.
Banks, S. A.
Berleu, H.
Braisted, M. P.
Bissell, G. W.
Bogardus, A.
Berlin, H.
Benedict, C. A.
Benedict, 2nd, W. G.
Bell, W. G.
Brusle, W. A.
Bischoff, H.
Cowles, G. W.
Corrie, W. E.
Crane, J. H.
Currie, M. A.
Denecke, F. W.
Fleet, A.
Franklin, J. B.
Fuller, B. W.
Fisher, P.
Frothingham, C. F,
Filley, F. C.
Foss, C. M.
Gowdey, W. H.
Gambling, W. M.
Godley, J. L.
Genin, E.
Gaddis, M. A.
Hyde, A. W.
Husted, G. M.
Harward, W. E.
Holbrook, J. W.
Haynes, M. C.
Hutchings, E W. Jr.
Hayden, A. L.
Hawley, C. L.
Hawkins, M T.
Isidor, S.
Jacobs, I.
Janncey, J. Jr.
Keefier, B. K.
Kingsland, E. A.
Kingsland, W. H.
Kappner, J. G.
Kellinger, S. M.

Lester, D. B.
Lane, J. H.
Linder, C F.
Moore, W. A.
Margary, T. S.
Mezzetti, G. W.
Martin, B. T.
McDonald, J.
Mitchell, J. M.
Maper, J. H.
Nixon, C. L.
Noe, A.
Noe, A A.
Prentiss, A. T.
Price, W. L.
Rink, P. A.
Rosenbaum, J. F.
Reed, R.
Romaine, W. A.
Richards, L. M.
Rackfeller, M. S.
Reynolds, M. T.
Schoonmaker, S. A.
Seligman, S.
Sullivan, T. J.
Selig, A.
Stew, L.
Stagers, E. N.
Samsou, J. D.
Sadler, T.
Skidmore, T. S.
Stroud, W. E.
Stewart, W.
Sargent, J.
Sutherland, M. T.
Schoonmaker. T. S.
Thomas, G. M.
Thorp, S. S.
Tucker, G.
Timolat, H. N.
Wood, J. W.
Whitehorn, W. A.
Webb, W.
Waldron, T. S.
Waterbury, M. V.
Yeaton, A. S.
Young, E. P.

HONORARY MEMBERS.

Alberts, W.
Bailey. S. B.
Burr, J. H.
Clough, Theo.
Cook, T. F.
Eckel, F.
Grain, F. Jr.
Halsted, W. P.
Johnson. J.
Kelly, R. J.
Kiersey, P. H.
Leon, M. J.
Millard, F.
Myers, G.
McGregor, J.
Nugent, P.
Petrie, H A.
Sayre, J. D.
Silva, John
Stokley, N. B.
Utter, E. D.
Watson, S. W.
White, C. E.
Wilcox, E. R.
Wilson, M. A.

SIXTH COMPANY.

Capt. R. M. Never,
1st Lieut, R. F. Halsted,
2nd "   Jos. B. Young,

Orderly, Geo. W. Ford,
2nd Sergt. C. G. Bartlett,
3rd   "   A. S. Brady,
4th   "   J. F. Ruggles,
5th   "   N. W. S. Catlin,
1st Corp'l, W. B. Freeman,
2nd   "   Chas Walke,
3rd   "   Gouv. Kemble, Jr.
4th   "   E. O. Bird,
Lance Corp'l, P. Schuyler, Jr.
    "   "   L. M. Carnes.

PRIVATES.

Alex. Annan,
Henry Arnold,
W. J. Bartow,
F. R. Bassett,
J. Benkard, Jr.
E. J. Birmingham,
A. H. Bissell,
E. Bowdoin,
Geo. Boyden,
J. H. Bradbury,
G. G. Brinckerhoff,
O. E. Brown,
C. S. Brown,
G. L. Browning,
O. J. Cambreleng,
Samuel Carey,
P. K. Chadwick,
Floyd Clarkson,
G. H. Coggeshall,
A. K. Cogswell,
Geo. S. Comstock,
H. M. Congdon,
W. Congdon,
Poinsett Cooper,
E. A. Cowdrey,
F. H. Cowdrey.
Edward Cozzens,
J. D. W. Cutting,
L. L. Cuvillier,
W. B. Dick,
Ritner Dock,
A. Douglas,
J. Duryee,
T. O. Ebaugh,
Geo. P. Edgar,
A. M. Elsworth,
J. B. Ezhardt,
Jno. Erving,
D. W. C. Falls,
G. C. Ferris,
C. E. Ford,
J. A. Foster,
J. E. Foster,
J. W. French,
W. C. Frost,
C. C. Gardiner,
E. L. Halsted,
Schuyler Hamilton,
F. Harrison,
J. H. H. Hawes,
J. E. Hayes,
P. Jaudon,
Elisha Jenkins,
Edward Kemp,
C. A. Kimball,
A. F. King,
R. King,
A. J. Lamb,
E. Laraque,
S. B. Lawrence,
W. H. Lawrence,
D. Marrenner,
J. McLaren,
J. J. McLaren,
A. McNulty,
G. L. Middlebrook,
L. H. Miller,
Geo. Palmer,
S. H. L. Rankin,

J. P. Raymond,
S. H. Robbins,
W. P. Roome,
T. P. Rowe,
W. P. Ryckman,
M. Ryder,
R. G. Shaw,
W. G. Shaw,
A. E. Sheldon,
O. G. Smedberg,
H. A. Still,
R. H. Stillwell,
W. A. Stoutenberg,
E. C. Sturges,
N. W. Stuyvesant, Jr.
C. T. Sutton,
H. Taylor,
H. T. Teer,
C. W. Thomae,
G. F. Thomae,
G. H. Thorpe,
J. W. Timpson,
C. H. Tomes,
F. A. T. Tracy,
W. W. Tracy,
F. C. Tucker,
W. E. Ulshoeffer,
E. W. Van Benschoten,
W. H. Vance,
C. F. Van Duzer,
W. R. Vermilye, Jr.
G. R. Vernon,
D. M. Walduck,
G. R. Watts,
Jas. Weeks,
E. N. West,
R. Weston,
F. A. Wheeler,
G. H. White,
W. T. Whiting,
Geo. W. Wilson,
F. M. Winston,
W. W. Winthrop,
W. S. Wood,
G. W. Young,
M. Young.

SEVENTH COMPANY.

Capt. John Monroe,
1st Lieut. J. P. Schemerhorn,
2nd   "   J. D. Moriarty,
1st Sergt. C. H. Winans,
2nd   "   E. S. Henry,
3rd   "   John L. Cameron,
4th   "   Chas. Hobbs, Jr.
5th   "   Geo. W. Eley,
1st Corpl. H. S. Bidwell,
2nd   "   R. H. Bowerman,
3rd   "   Thomas E. Delano,
4th   "   Jno. J. Coger,
1st Lance Cor. J. H. W. Kemp,
2nd   "   "   Thos. R. Gooch,
3rd   "   "   W. H. Smith,
4th   "   "   E. M. Felt.

PRIVATES.

Allcoke, R. S.
Anderson, J. W.
Annable, Thos. H.
Avery, John
Barker, L. E.
Barnes, C. C.
Bennett, A. C. W.
Bennett, C. F.
Bogert, A. Schuyler
Bootman, R. W.
Breck, C. J.
Brittone, H. H.
Brittone, E.

Callendar, W. E.
Chatfield, H. S.
Chevalier, Geo.
Clarke, J. L.
Collins,
Cortelyou, P. C.
Crane, E. S.
Cravy,
Curtis, Robert E.
Delano, J.
Delamaiter, C. H.
Donaldson, E.
Drew, W.
Dunscombe, J. H U.
Duryee. W. B. C.
Easton, B. C.
Eddy, E. Jr.
Ely, Jos. W. Jr.
Fitch, G. R.
Fowler, D. H.
Gibson, R. P.
Gibson, W. H.
Godfrey, P. C.
Hall, Chas.
Hart, H.
Hathaway, T. E.
Hartwell,
Hayden, J. T.
Hewett,
Holdridge D. H.
Holmes, Geo. F. Jr.
Hornell, A. J.
Howe,
Hughes,
Hutchins,
Ingersoll,
Klanbey, A.
Laudnback, D. Jr.
Lent, N. H.
Lent, W. H.
Matthews, H. E.
McClenachan, C. T.
McDonough, L. R.
McKesson, J.
McJimsey, Eugene,
Mealey, P. J.
Meachan. Geo. G.
Moise, B. V.
Montauge, H. W.
Moon, Geo. G.
Money,
O'Brien, F. J.
Oliver, Richard
Oliver, J. W.
Oldershaw, R.
Olmstead,
Pinckney, F. H.
Pomeroy, A. H.
Putnam. E. T.
Risley, L. S.
Robinson,
Schemerhorn, Chas. A.
Schemerhorn, L.
Schemerhorn, W. H.
Schram,
Sherman, S. J.
Simpson, W.
Smith, A. J.
Smith, R. B.
Steers, A.
Steers, F. J.
Simons, A. H.
Skellern, Geo. W.
Stetson, N.
Stetson, N. Jr.
Stewart, A. R.
Stewart, R. K.
Stone, W.
St. John, W.
Tallmadge,
Tallman, Geo. H
Tiffany, H. D.

Tiffany, Layman
Thompson, S. W.
Thorpe, R. A.
Trotter, E. A.
Trotter, F. E.
Tufts, W. Fuller
Turnbull, Geo. R.
Turner, W.
Van Loan, B. F.
Van Benschoten, M.
Vanderweider,
Wheelright, W. G.
Williamson, C.

C. S. Graffulla, Musical Director of the Band.
David Graham, Drum Major.

EIGHTH COMPANY.

Capt. Henry C. Shumway.
1st Lieut. Chas. B. Bostock,
2nd   "   Chas. B. Babcock,
1st Sergt. Jno. W. Spicer,
2nd   "   Sam'l W. Sears,
3rd   "   Edwd. O. Kettle,
4th   "   Henry D. Green,
5th   "   Wm. L. M. Burger,
Commissary, Ex. Sgt. Gilbert L. Arrowsmith,
1st Corp, Gould B. Hedenberg,
2nd   "   Chas. E. Mears,
3rd   "   Benjamin Loder, Jr.

PRIVATES.

Allen, Wm. B.
Austen, David E.
Allen, Chas. D.
Abrams, Jas. C.
Arms, C. Ernst,
Baker, John M.
Barbey, Adolphus H.
Bassett, Wm. H.
Bearnes, Jos. H.
Beecher, H. C.
Bredt, Ernest
Brown, Ed. S.
Brown, Wm. H.
Burdett, Geo. F.
Burkhalter, Jno. H.
Burkhalter, Stephen Jr.
Buckley,
Blake, Clarence A.
Barry, Robt. P.
Brownell, S. B.
Baker, Jas. T.
Casey, Jas. S.
Cozzens, Thos. M.
Coles, W. H. Jr.
Cargill, Frank
Champion, Chas. P.
Crockett, John A.
Davidson, Albert
Denison, Lyman, Jr.
Denison, Chas. S.
Daskin, Jas. W.
Easton, Alfred H.
Eager, Peter
Ellis, W. Irving
Farrell, Wm. R.
Field, Robt. M. Jr.
Field, Saml. B.
Flagg, Montague
Ford, Robt. O. N.
Foster, S. B.
Gouge, Edwd. H.
Grant, Jas. B.
Gansevoort, Henry S.
Green, Frank W.
Gifford, S. R.

Grant, T. C.
Grant, F. H.
Herrick, Elias J.
Hertzel, Geo. W.
Hillman, Jno. S.
Howe, Augustus
Howell, Wm. P.
Hurlbut, Wm. H.
Hubbell, Henrp W. Jr.
Hull, Jno. Henry
Hall, Robt. L. S.
Hollister, Henry H.
Hay,
Haff,
Hastin, P.
Jacobson, Wm. G.
Jaudon, Frank
Johnson, Ebenezer R.
Jung, Chas. T.
Keine, John P.
Keese, J Lawrence—Accidently shot dead while in camp.
Lamb, Joseph
Leveridge, A. De Witt
Lewis, Thompson
Lane, J. Remsen
Lapsley, Howard
Levick,
Macy, Theo. E.
Marvine, Wm. H.
Mather, De Witt C.
Meeks, Albert V.
Moller, Wm. H.
Morgan, Jno. W.
Morrison, Jas. Jr.
Morrison, Wm. A.
Muller, Adrian H. Jr.
Murfey, Geo. W.
Murfey, John H.
Mayer, Saml. D.
McMillan, Alex.
McKee,
Murray, Wm. S.
Mabee, Foster N.
Murray, Geo. W.
Mason, Albert
Moss, Cortland D.
Moran, Edward
Mansfield, W. D.
Neilson, Edwd. N.
Oley, John H.
Owen, Wm. H.
Pomeroy,
Parisort, Ernest J.
Parmelee, Lewis C.
Phillips, Henry J.
Price, Chas. W.
Polhamus, Henry A.
Pease, Walter A.
Paterson, W. G.
Pearce, Chas. E.
Peat, C. B.
Peat, F. T.
Robinson, Jas. E.
Rollinson, Saml. O.
Rollinson,
Ryder, Alfred V.
Reeve, Ch.
Rogers, Edmond P.
Rushton, R. C.
Bogers, Philip C.
Richardson, Geo. R.
Rankin,
Spear, P. B.
Stevenson,
Smith, Lewis B.
Spear, Edwin
Spencer, Piere, F.
Smith, E. A. W., Ex. 1st Lieut. of Company H.
Trowbridge, Joe. A.
Talcott, E. N. Kirk

Van Rett, Saml. K.
Williams, Geo. C.
Wilson, Henry S. Jr.
Wood, Alexander G.
Willis, John O.
Whitehouse, Edwd. M.
Wethabee,
Welch,
Wood, T. H.
Webber, J. T.

NINTH COMPANY, ARTILLERY.

1st Lieu't, H. A. Cragin,
2nd   "   C. C. White,
Orderly Sgt., J. H. Macbride,
2   "   H. J. Fuller,
3   "   Edwin Reeler, Jr.
4   "   "Lawr'ce Moore, Jr.

PRIVATES.

Andrews, G. D.
Arthur, H. E.
Barie, James
Baker, Joshua
Barrett,
Barney, N. C.
Ball, C. J. C.
Brownirl, Henry
Brainard, L. W.
Bramhall, W. L.
Beirne, James A.
Bugle, Benedick
Buch, Theo. H.
Carman, Richard
Church, E. D.
Coan, W. B.
Concklin, J. R. Jr.
Concklin, J. K.
Carey, R. P.
Coombs, Philip
Cumming, A. M.
Dayton, G. E.
Davis, G. C.
Davies, Barry
Dean, W. L.
Doughty, G. R.
Dunnel, G. H.
Derbeu, J. P. Jr.
Durfee, Fenton
Eddy, Clinton
Edgar, S. P.
Ellis, Franklin
Farmer, George
Fisher, W. N.
Fitzpatrick, Thomas
Fordred,
Franklin, D. R.
Giberson, S.
Goodrich, L. O.
Greaves, E. E.
Harmstead, R. M.
Howell, J. R.
Knaps, E. S.
King, C. E.
Law, R J.
Lockwood, G. A.
Lord, J. R.
Leuezy, Joseph
Mack, Valentine
Manning, J.
Marlor, G.
Matthews, James
Martin, P. R.
McCrea, J. E.
McDonald, Alex.
McLane, Arch'd
Merchant, A. T.
Merriman, E. R.
Miller, B. B.

SUPPLEMENTARY NOTE.

CHRONICLES

OF

THE REBELLION

OF

1861,

FORMING A

Complete History of the Secession Movement

FROM ITS COMMENCEMENT,

TO WHICH ARE ADDED THE

MUSTER ROLL OF THE UNION ARMY,

AND

EXPLANATORY AND ILLUSTRATIVE NOTES OF THE LEADING FEATURES OF THE CAMPAIGN.

BY CHARLES J. ROSS.

SOLD BY ALL BOOKSELLERS AND NEWSDEALERS.

New-York:

FRANK McELROY, PRINTER, 113 NASSAU STREET.

1861.

BUSINESS NOTICES.

CANTON TEA WAREHOUSE, 260 GREENWICH ST.

In times like the present, when there is not only a dearth of employment, but a scarcety of the "circulating medium," it becomes every one to regulate their household upon principles of the strictest economy, and in making their purchases, to obtain the *best* and *cheapest* commodities.

It is a maxim in commercial circles that "the cheapest goods are the best." We had, for a time, a doubt of the truth of this statement, but a proof of the Wares vended by Mr. Thomas R. Agnew, at his establishment, as noted above, fully convinced us of our error. We have made a trial of several of the Goods in which he deals, and are enabled to classify them as the *very best*, whilst in point of price they can not be under-quoted in the city. This remark applies to his large stocks of Sugar, Tea, Coffee and Molasses. Being an importer, and purchasing for cash, Mr. Agnew can, therefore, supply his customers upon unusually advantageous terms. GROCERIES, TEAS, WINES, PROVISIONS, &c., &c., are in store in large abundance, and every housewife who would desire to economise should not fail to patronize the

CANTON TEA WAREHOUSE, 260 GREENWICH ST.

ACCOUTREMENTS FOR OUR JUVENILE SOLDIERS!

STRASBURGER & NUHN, 65 MAIDEN LANE.

Loyalty to the Stars and Stripes is now the order of the day. Children are the creatures of imitation, and hence the streets of this great city are daily perambulated by them in all the gay and attractive uniforms of the several Regiments of Volunteers who have gone forth to give Jefferson Davis's legions a specimen of their military capacity, their courage and their daring, and to convince them that "the Union Must and Shall be Maintained." But although the juvenile would-be soldier has obtained his uniform, he wants something more in order to be fully equipped: these are what are termed in military phraseology, "Accoutrements." Having examined the various establishments in the city where Juvenile Military Accoutrements are to be had, we have no hesitation in recommending that of the firm whose name is given in our heading. There can be had the "army sword," with all its trappings, plain and ornamental. The musket and bayonet fashioned according to the most approved rifle bore, or latest Enfield pattern. Haversacks, calculated to hold a three *hours'* rations, and knapsacks, furnished in all that the juvenile warrior requires, are constantly on sale. Another necessary appendage is the drum; by its roll the young forces are gathered in, and by its tap the science of marching is acquired. Then, again, the tiny bugle is to be had in every style and variety. In a word, there is not a single article which the youthful "son of mars" requires to equip him for actual service that is not to be had at this establishment. The character of the house is such as to impart confidence that the articles are of the best quality, whilst the excellent trade facilities of the principals, both at home and abroad, ensure that their stock can be vended at the lowest cash prices of the day. The house of Messrs. Strasburger & Nuhn can be truly recommended as the best of the class in the city, where customers will be politely received and their orders filled with promptness and despatch.

Pastime in the Camp and the Social Circle.

A. DOUGHERTY, 26 Beekman Street.

"All work and no play makes Jack a dull boy." This is a saying no less ancient than it is truthful. The mind as well as the body requires relaxation; consequently various means have been devised to effect an object so desirable. Among the many plans of amusement, is that of Card Playing. In the camp, it is the favorite pastime after the duties of the day have been performed. One of the last things which the Volunteer attends to before his march is to supply himself with a few packs of the best playing cards. He knows that they will wile away many an hour which would otherwise be irksome and tedious. Hence, the enquiry "Where can I get the *best* and *cheapest* Cards?" We have several manufacturers in th's country. At the head of the business stands Mr. A. DOUGHERTY, 26 Beekman Street, in this city. Being practically engaged in the business for a long series of years, his styles are unlimited, and the quality of each such as to give universal satisfaction. A comparison of Mr. Dougherty's Cards with the celebrated productions of De La Rue, of London, will convince any one that for strength, neatness of design and beauty of finish, they are without a compeer, whilst in the matter of price we believe they are the cheapest in the market. Just now Mr. Dougherty has produced a new pattern which he calls the "Union." We have examined this class of his Cards, and are enabled to pronounce it superior in every respect. It only requires to be seen to be admired, and its excellent quality appreciated. Certain we are that when fully known every soldier of our brave army will yearn to have a supply in his knapsack. But Cards are favorites in the family circle. Here, too, the Union design must be a universal favorite. Dealers and retailers of Cards should bear this in mind, and lay in a supply, as the stock will sell like "hot cakes."

SOLDIERS SPECIAL NOTICE.—Do your duty towards yourselves, protect your health, use HOLLOWAY'S PILLS and OINTMENT. For Wounds, Sores, Bowel Complaints and Fevers, they are a perfect safeguard. Full directions how to use them with every b x. Only 25 Cents.

THE CRISIS.

As general Scott is Commander-in-Chief of the United States forces, now in the field against the rebels, so also is Barker Generalissimo in the Grand Army of Ale Venders. From him you can obtain the best Ales of the day, all drawn from the wood. A large glass for 3 cents. Barker is also sole agent for Threlfalls celebrated English Ales. Note the address, GOLDEN ALE VAULTS, No. 2 Tryon Row.

The Roll of the Union Army.

THE SIXTY-NINTH REGIMENT OF THE N. Y. S. M.

This patriotic and courageous band of heroes merits an early notice. As the reader is aware, it is composed of Irishmen mostly, all of whom are adopted citizens. Their commander, Colonel Corcoran, is a universal favorite among his men, and the popularity of the regiment is attested on every occasion when it turns out by the loud and universal plaudits with which it is greeted by the populace at large. The Sixty-ninth was one of the earliest of the New York State Militia to start for the National Capital. Whenever an Irishman appears on the field of battle, he is sure to give undeniable evidence of undaunted heroism, and nothing could exceed the zeal with which he throws himself into the conflict. This remark is particularly applicable to the Sixty-ninth, from the moment they set out upon the march to Washington until their return from Bull Run.

When the news of the attack on the Sixth Massachusetts Regiment became known, the Sixty-ninth Regiment announced their readiness for the field; and, had the government permitted it, the total strength of the corps would have been 2,000 strong. As it was, the whole force at Bull Run was over thirteen hundred rank and file. The departure of the Sixty-ninth was made the occasion of a grand turn-out. The line of march through Broadway and the other streets through which they passed on the way to the steamer, at the foot of Cortlandt street, was one grand ovation—every one seemed desirous of marking with unqualified approbation such a prompt response to the call of the government. The Sixty-ninth formed in Great Jones street, the right resting on Broadway. Long before the troops made their appearance, the neighboring thoroughfares were completely choked up with people to catch a glimpse—perhaps a last one—of the familiar faces of friends and relatives before they should embark. The rush for positions in the regiment was tremendous, and thousands who had been enrolled were left behind, in consequence of the orders of the Major-General that not more than one thousand men, all told, should be taken from the city.

The Phœnix Brigade performed escort duty.

They numbered about six hundred men. They had a brass field-piece, belonging to the engineer corps of the regiment, which they continued to fire at intervals throughout the line of march. A large company of firemen, members of 18 Truck, who volunteered their services to the colonel for special police duty, worked the gun, under the direction of one of Captain Kirker's company of Engineers. All along Broadway the surging tide of human beings displayed the utmost enthusiasm. Wild hurrahs, clapping of hands, and the waving of handkerchiefs was to be heard and seen from the windows and balconies and the crowded sidewalks of Broadway. The men of the Sixty-ninth received their ovation with becoming dignity. They saluted all whom they recognized; but it was evident that they felt they were marching on a serious errand, and that not a few were never again to return. So densely packed was the route that the regiment was obliged to march in file. Some five hundred men who had been left out determined to follow their favorite regiment as long as possible, and accompanied them all the way to the boat. It was 5, P. M., April 23, when the Sixty-ninth reached pier No. 4, North river, and there a scene of the most exciting character took place. In every direction people had taken up positions in the rigging of vessels; they covered the tops of the pier sheds and houses, and every place where a view could be obtained. Here the cheering was vociferous in the extreme.

The regiment was sadly disappointed on finding that it would not be marched through Baltimore; for it was their darling hope that they would have an opportunity of punishing in the most terrible manner the bloodthirsty cowards of that city who had, on the previous Friday, interrupted the march of the Sixth Massachusetts Regiment, then on its way to Washington.

What rendered the departure of the Sixty-ninth a great popular event was the fact of its colonel having been court-martialed for refusing to parade his regiment in honor of the Prince of Wales. The Irish portion of the people of this country have strong prejudices against the royal family of England. They fancy that to it can be traced no small portion of the political grievances which prevail in their native land. It forms no part of duty to inquire into the validity of such opinions; at the same time, it is nothing more than justice to Queen Victoria to say that no monarch has ever occupied the British throne who showed a greater desire to promote the best interests of the people of Ireland. Bad and tyrannical landlords there are, and will be, in that country; but for this the royal family cannot be held accountable. Col. Corcoran is one of those genuine Irish spirits who adopted heart and soul the memorable social aphorism uttered by the late Mr. Drummond, when under-Secretary at Dublin Castle — viz.: "Property has its duties as well as its rights." He was brought up in a part of Ireland—the county of Sligo—where he had good opportunity of studying the landlord grievances of his country. Having entered the Irish Constabulary, he was located in the county of Donegal—a part of the country where all his national sympathies on behalf of his oppressed countrymen were called forth. Col. Corcoran has always been an ardent lover of civil and religious liberty. This circumstance had no small share in inducing him to leave Ireland in 1849, and settle down in this city. The history of his connection with the Sixty-ninth may be briefly told. He rose from the ranks, having joined the regiment as a private in Company I, Captain John Judge. His election as colonel took place on the 25th of August, 1859. His subsequent career has fully justified the choice of his men, and brought the discipline and drill of his command to a state of perfection which hardly a militia regiment in the country can lay claim to.

In the peculiar qualifications essential to a successful military commander Col. Corcoran is amply endowed. His family—an ancient and respectable one—have had a taste for the profession of arms. His father—Thomas Corcoran, we believe—was an officer in the British army, and served with much distinction in the West Indies. Besides, in early life the colonel was brought up in an excellent school for calling out all the military genius which he possessed, and developing in all its pristine vigor that principle of manly courage and noble daring which he displayed on the battle-field at Bull Run.

But while justly proud, as the country must be, of Col. Corcoran, as commander of the Sixty-ninth, it must not be supposed that his officers and men lacked in loyalty and devotion to the United States. It is true that some one or two of the men refused to take the oath of allegiance on being mustered into the service of the United States. Col. Corcoran set at rest any suspicion of want of

courage and loyalty on the part of his regiment by his letter, dated Georgetown Heights, May 10, 1861, wherein he states:

"Once for all, in reply to various intimations and inquiries, each more or less disparagingly implying an uncertainty as to the loyalty and military spirit of the regiment under my command, I beg leave to state, and do so positively and finally, that the Sixty-ninth Regiment N. Y. S. M., has come on here in prompt compliance with the call of the President of the United States, in defending the national sovereignty, property, and flag, and that wherever, and whenever the National Government, established and acting at Washington, may order the Sixty-ninth, there and then the Sixty-ninth are resolved and sworn, to a man, to act. Holding, as they do, that they are no longer citizens and soldiers of the State of New York, but are unreservedly and heartily citizens and solders of the United States of America, of which President Lincoln is the legitimate Executive, and the stars and stripes are, the world over, the recognized, historic, and inviolable symbol, after this declaration, the Sixty-ninth will make no answer to and take no notice of any such doubts or imputations as those in question, save and except what their military obligations in camp or battle will enable them to give."

Now, this was published at a time when the Sixty-ninth Regiment were by no means treated as they ought to have been by the Commissariat Department at Washington. Their food was not merely deficient in quantity, but was inferior in quality. This fact was commented upon at the time by some of the public journals of the day. One paper, of the 20th of May, contains the following: "During the past week, repeated complaints, verbal and written, have reached this office. In one case, we are told that the gallant Sixty-ninth have been exposed to privations and hardships which the most miserable outcast in the wilds of Connaught would not have to endure. * * * The pauper who is quartered in the almshouse—the criminal "serving his term" in the State prison, or the vagrant sent to rusticate on Blackwell's Island—are fed and clothed sufficiently so as to preserve health and strength. Here are men who enlist to fight their country's battles, who leave their families and their homes to uphold the Constitution and its laws, who are so badly treated that we wonder they are fit for any kind of military duty. The Sixty-ninth, we are told, were frequently compelled to make mother earth their bed, and from damps and chills exposed to the liability of contracting illness which would compel them to retire from the service." For all this, the Sixty-ninth bore up with undoniable courage; and if hard work was to be performed, they were sure to be the foremost in its performance. Their march from Annapolis to Washington was harrassing in the extreme, and when they arrived at Georgetown Heights, they had only to commence their military labors *de novo*. The erection of their works named Fort Corcoran, in honor of their colonel, were a wonder and a model to nearly every other regiment, and pronounced by the highest military authorities perfection itself. Earnestly and unceasingly did they labor in the trenches, whilst they had more than full share of picket duty and daily drills. The word fear was wiped out of their vocabulary, and to murmur or repine at all the tasks allotted them was considered by the humblest private derogatory to the character of the true soldier.

When Gen. Scott determined upon the advance towards Manassas Junction, it was assigned to the Sixty-ninth that it should form the "advance guard"—a strong proof of the superior excellence of both colonel, officers and men. Nor was the trust misplaced. Nobly did they lead the federal army on to that bloody field at Bull Run, where, after a long and wearied march through a broiling sun and bad and dusty roads, and without food or sustenance of almost any kind, they opened the battle on the 21st of July. Of the character of the achievements of the Sixty-ninth on that memorable day, this is not the place to dilate. It will be found in the regular historical part of these volumes. Suffice it to say, that every charge was made in gallant style, and although it was made with fearful loss, it cut the enemy to pieces.

Notwithstanding all the temptations to which the Sixty-ninth was exposed, there was a perfect freedom from anything like excess. The men, one and all, attended to the spiritual advice of the reverend chaplain, Father Mooney, who was endeared to every member of the regiment. He was in truth, the soldiers' friend, and contributed in no small degree to nerve the men for the great conflict which took place.

While every man who loves the country must deplore the heavy loss which this gallant band of heroes sustained, it is with pride that they can look back upon the daring deeds of Corcoran, the lamented Haggerty, and the indomitable courage of Meagher. Their names and every other, officer and man, of the regiment, will be treasured up for generations yet unborn, and a country's gratitude speak trumpet-tongued in praise of their patriotism and military efficiency. Let the reader now turn to the muster-roll of the Sixty-ninth, contemplate its bloody record, and earnestly pray that the great disposer of all events may, in his infinite wisdom, restore peace and harmony to the land.

Muster Roll of the Sixty-ninth Regiment, N. Y. S. M.

REGIMENTAL STAFF.

Colonel .... Michael Corcoran.*
Lt. Colonel .... Robert Nugent.
Major .... Alderman James Bagley.†
Adjutant.................... ...... John McKeon.
Chaplain...... .... Rev. Thomas Mooney.
Engineer....................... James B. Kirker.
Surgeon.................... ... Dr Kiernan
Quartermaster.................. James B. Tully.
Paymaster.................... Matthew Kehol.

* Wounded at Bull Run, and taken prisoner.

† This officer did not accompany the regiment to the seat of war, and was not engaged in any action with the enemy.

NON-COMMISSIONED STAFF.

Sergeant Major.................... Arthur Tracey
            (Wounded in action.)
Quartermaster-Sergeant.............. John Bell
Ordinance Sergeant.................... F. Page
First Color-Bearer................ John Murphy
   (Wounded and prisoner at Richmond.)
Second Color-Bearer............. James Reilly
   (Deserted and fled from the enemy.)
Right General Guide......... Thomas Sweeny
Left General Guide............ . Robert Eagan
Corporals of Color Guard { ..Patrick O'Hearn
                         { ....J. W. Herbert
                         { ......John Canoll
Hospital Steward.................. John Murray
Drum Major.................. Maurice Murphy
Principal Musician........ Thomas Monaghan

COMPANY A.

Captain, John Haggerty.
1st Lieut., Theo. Kelly.
2d   "   Daniel Strane.
3d   "   Daniel Sullivan.
1st Sergt., And'w Birmingham.
2d   "   Patrick Gunny.
3d   "   Michael Brennan.
4th   "   John Fahy
5th   "   James Kilcher.
1st Corp'l, John Lynch.
2d   "   Patrick Walsh.
3d   "   Thomas Sullivan.
4th   "   Richard Murray.
5th   "   Patrick Cahill.
1st Drummer, M. E. Hill.
2d   "   Richard Bell.

PRIVATES.

Angle, Thomas G.
Byrne, William
Bracken, James
Buody, Philip
Burke, Redmond
Boylan, Thomas
Bowen, Chas.
Brennan, J. W.
Brown, Thomas
Brodie, Patrick
Carr, James
Cleary, William
Carolin, Alexander
Claffery, Michael
Crosby, Charles
Crowly. Daniel
Carrol, James
Cummings, Joseph
Clancey, Miles C.
Corcoran, Michael
Cahil, D. J.
Cannery, W. H.
Daly, John
Draddy, Daniel
Downey, John
Dilks, Joseph C.
Doheny, John C.
Dooley, Patrick
Dunn, Peter
Dunn, John
Duffy, Hugh
Dunn, Joseph
Dunnigan, Michael
Duffy, Owen J.
Duncan, William
Egan, Thomas
Faniell, Thomas F.
Fagan, Matthew
Finigan, Patrick
Fogarty, John
Ford, George
Fitzgerald, Michael
Findley, John
Flynn, Peter
Fencer, Thomas
Gately, Thomas
Galligher, Neil
Gaffney, John
Gilder, Francis
Groves, Robert
Gaynor, Patrick
Gerity, William
Hanlon, Edward
Henney, Robert
Hetherington, John
Hughes, John
Kelly, Michael
Kelly, Richard A.
Kelly, Richard C.
Kelly, Robert
Kelly, William
Kennedy, Patrick J.
Keilan, Thomas
Kiernan, James
King, John
Lilly, Patrick
Looney, John J.
Mackin, James
Morgan, Martin
McCain, John
McDermot, Luke
McDonough, John
McGiving, Michael
McNaery, Alexander
Mullen, John
Mulvihill, Thomas
McLaughlin, Patrick
Murphy, Hugh
McSweeny, Miles
Montgomery, Thomas
Myers, Daniel
Monaghan, Martin
McTague, Hugh
Murphy, William
Murphy, Maurice
Mulhoony, John
Norris, Thomas D.
Newcombe, James
O'Farrell, Patrick
O'Donnel, Michel
O'Callaghan, William
O'Hara, Joseph
O'Neile, Patrick
O'Shaughnessy, William
Peters, Jeremiah
Page, Robert
Robinson, James
Reynolds, Bernard
Reynolds, John
Reed, Michael H.
Rooney, James
Rogers, James P.
Ryan, John
Sann, Edward F.
Sheldrick, Thomas
Shephard, William
Shea, John
Star, Patrick
Sullivan John

KILLED.

Capt. J. H. Haggerty.
Charles Crossley, }
John Dunn, and   } Privates.
Patrick Lilley, }

WOUNDED.

Sergeant James.
Kilcher, Corporal
Patrick Cahill,
William Duncan,
Thomas Egan,
William Finnigan,   } Privates.
Patrick Flannigan,
Richard A. Kelly,
Rich'd C. Kelly, and
Joseph O'Hara,
The latter was left on the
field at Bull Run for dead, but
has since recovered.

PRISONERS.

Thomas Brown.
John Gaffney.*
Thomas Montgomery.
John Mulrooney.
Jeremiah Peters.*
Bernard Reynolds.*
Owen J. Duffy.

* These men were also severely wounded in action.

COMPANY B.

Commandant, Wm. M. Giles.
1st Lieut., Thomas Leddy.
2d Lieut, Laurence Cahill,
1st Sergt , M. P. Bowman.
2d   "   Richard Dunn.
3d   "   George Donavan.
4th   "   Thomas Moore.
5th   "   Patrick Nevins.
1st Corp'l, Thomas Kiernan.
2d   "   Wm. Pannington.
3d   "   Philp A. McMahon.
4th   "   Patrick Minegnole.
1st Music'n, Bern'd McFadden.
2d   "   Thos. McFadden.

PRIVATES.

Butler, George
Beine, Michael
Barret, Patrick
Boyle, Thomas
Brady, John
Banan, James
Bergen, Michael
Berne, Matthew
Brooks, James
Brady, Peter
Brown, Philip
Caffery, William
Canavan, Charles
Coffe, John
Coleman, John
Cline, Michael
Cline, Thomas
Collins, Michael
Conavan, Andrew
Cronin, Timothy
Cullin, John
Dillon, John P.
Dillon, Thomas
Donelley, William
Donelley, Francis
Donelley, Martin
Dougherty, William
Doyle, Patrick
Dunn, Patrick
Duyer, Robert
Flagherty, Simon

Flynn, Patrick
Gallagher, Bernard
Gallagher, John
Gibbons, Michael
Gleason, William
Glenn, William
Hagan, Francis
Hart, John
Haslip, George
Joice, William
Kelly, Arthur
Kelly, Edward
Kelly, James
Lally, John
Lanargan, John
Leddy, John
Leonard, James
McCabe, Alexander
McCaffery, Thomas
McCormick, Peter
McGuire, Laurence
McGuiness, James
McGuik, James
McGuik, Andrew
McGovern, Thomas
McKenna, Patrick
McHugh, John
McManus, Thomas
McManus, Hugh
McManus, Laurence
McNeill, John T.
McLaughlin, John
McKnight, Daniel
McTeague, John
Meadows, Richard
Meyers, William
Moore, William
Maddin, Patrick, Jr.
Manley, Patrick
Moore, William, 1st
Moore, William, 2d
Martin, Thomas
Martin, Thomas G.
Martin, Patrick
Mullin, Christopher
Murphy, Peter
Murphy, Joseph
Neeper, Thomas F.
O'Brien, Dennis
O'Connor, Patrick
O'Keefe, Michael
O'Shea, Michael.
Quin, Michael
Reilly, Patrick
Reilly, Phillip
Reynolds, Michael
Roath, Oswald
Rogers, William
Scott, John
Scanlon. Timothy
Shaw, George
Shuter, Richard
Smith, James
Smith, Owen
Sullivan, Dennis
Sullivan, Edward
Sullivan, William F.
Thornton, John
Walsh, William
Watson, Kiernan

KILLED.

Doyle, Luke
O'Donnel, Patrick
Shorton, Denis
Sheridan, Daniel

WOUNDED.

Kiernan, T. (Corporal.)
Shuter, Richard (Corporal.)

Cullen, John
Reilly, Patrick

PRISONERS AT RICHMOND.

Kier, John
Nugent, John
Joyce, William
McGuiness, James
McNeill, John T.
McTague, John
Murphy, Peter

MISSING, SUPPOSED TO BE KILLED.

Moore, William
Scott, John

COMPANY C.

Captain, James Cavannagh.
1st Lieut., James J. Smith.
2nd   "   Michael O'Keiff.
3rd   "   Jasper M. Whitty.
1st Sergt., Michael O'Connor.
2nd   "   Patrick Keatinge.
3rd   "   William Allen.
4th   "   Pierce McHenry.
5th   "   Carthage Lyons.
1st Corp'l, Timothy Carr.
2nd   "   Patrick Price.
3rd   "   Michael Fitzgerald.
4th   "   Lysird.

MUSICIANS.

1st, George Decker.
2nd, John Degraw.
3rd, James Brenan.

PRIVATES.

Armstrong, Phoenix
Brady, Matthew
Brown, Michael
Burnes, James A.
Burnes, William
Callaghan, Cornelius
Callaghan, Michael
Callan, Thomas
Comber, Ganett
Concklio, James
Connell, Philip
Carley, John
Coogan, John
Corcoran, Andrew
Cuddy, James
Cummins, Timothy W.
Curly, Peter
Daly, John
Daun, Bryan
Davis, Thomas
Dolan, Thomas
Davauny, Owen
Donnelly, Patrick
Donnovan, Cornelius
Donnovan, Daniel
Doran, Valentine
Duffy, Thomas
Egan, John
Egan, Michael
Fagan, Christopher
Fagan, John
Farmer, John
Fitzgerald, Patrick—1st
Fitzgerald, Patrick—2nd
Fobey, Patrick
Fonestal, William
Gallagher, Barclay

Galiven, John
Hattigan, Michael
Mammell, Peter
Healy, Richard H.
Helden, Michael
Himes, Jones
Higgins, Michael
Holly, Edward
Hodgins, George
Hinly, Michael
Jacobs, Benjamin
Johnston, Edward
Johnston, Josita
Keett, John
Kennedy, Daniel
Lacy, Thomas
Leahy, James
Leahy, William
Limrahan, Patrick
Long, Michael J.
McDonald, Thomas
McGorath, Edward
McGuinness, Sylvester
McHugh, John
McLaughlin, William
McLarkey, Patrick
McMahon, Arthur
McManus, John
McQuade, Thomas
McNamara, Martin
Moran, Patrick H.
Moore, William
Murphy, Michael H.
Murphy, Menthus
Muneny, Daniel
Munay, James
O'Donnel, James
O'Niell, Gregory
O'Reilly, Thomas
Palmer, Frederick
Racey, Robert H.
Regan, James
Reilly, Bernard
Reilly, Charles
Ryan, John—No. 1.
Ryan, John—No. 2.
Scott, Frank P.
Shannon, Philip
Shaw, Robert
Spelman, James
Stark, Thomas
Sullivan, Dennis
Sullivan, Michael
Sullivan, Patrick
Sweeny, Michael
Troy, William
Welsh, David
Welsh, Lawrence
Williams, Edward
Woods, John
Wynne, James

KILLED.

Hugh Reynolds.

WOUNDED.

Timothy Carr, at Bull Run, and not since heard of.

MISSING.

Thomas F. Kenny,
Patrick Blake,
Arthur Kelly,
Patrick Logan,
Nelhy William,
Michael Kerrigan.

DESERTED, MAY 15.

John Brady,
Thomas Carr.

COMPANY D. *

Captain, Thos. Clarke.
1st Lieut., Thomas Fay.
2d   "   Richard Dalton.
3d   "   Martin Hoyle.
1st Sergt., Michael Maguire.
2d   "   Patrick Goodman.
3d   "   John Murphy
4th   "   Chas. Ghegan.
1st Corpl., John O'Brien.
2d   "   John Jackson.
3d   "   John O'Brien.
    "   Martin Ryan.
Drummer, Michael Corcoran.

PRIVATES.

Ahern, Michael
Brown, John
Brackly, Edward J.
Bowes, John
Ramon, Chas.
Buck, Stephen
Brady, Patrick
Collins, James
Canoll, Henry
Cavannagh, Wm.
Cox, John
Cullin, Felix
Cummings, John
Casa, William
Colgan, Matthew
Campbell, John
Chambers, Henry
Cullan, Edward
Callanan, Patrick
Callanan, Thomas
Dunellan, Patrick
Darcy, Thomas
Daly, Peter F.
Davis, Henry W.
Dona, Thomas
Dugan, Joseph
Dunigan, Michael
Cagen, Patrick
English, Patrick
Ewin, Owen
Foley, George
Fisher, Hugh O.
Finhant, Nelson
Fitzimmons, Richard
Green, John
Gaynor, Thomas
Grant, Donald
Gardiner, Robert
Galvin, John
Hammood, Robert
Heaney, James
Heaney, Francis
Hayes, John, Jr.
Hughes, John, Sen.
Hanley, Michael
Kerley, James
King, Edward
Manning, Wm.
Mitchell, Thos.
Moloney, Michael
Monaghan, Denis
Mooney, Philip J.
Morrisey, Edward
Murray, Terence
Mulligan, James
Maher, William
McCannon, Francis
Murphy, Daniel
Murphy, John
Murphy, Michael

* Extracted from the Paymaster's Roll—no other source of information being available.

Murphy, Michael C.
McCabe, Bernard
McCauly, Thomas
McClusky, Geo.
McDermott, Patrick
McDonald, Patrick
McGill, James
McGrath, Michael
McGuin, James
McKenna, John
McManus, Bernard
McShawe, John
O'Brien, Thomas
O'Daly, Edmund J.
O'Keefe, Daniel
O'Lorn, Hugh F.
O'Neil, Michael
O'Rourke, Patrick
Oates, Bernard
Punch, Patrick J.
Quirk, Thomas
Quinn, Thomas
Redman, Michael W.
Ready, James
Reynolds, Thomas
Reardon, Timothy
Shiel, Lawrence
Shea, Jeremiah
Shanley, Thomas
Shehan, Timothy
Slevin, Thomas
Sullivan. John
Sullivan, Michael
Trainor. Michael
Walsh, John
Walsh, Michael
Wimbs, Thomas
White, John

COMPANY E.

Captain, Patrick Kelly.
1st Lieut., John Bagley.
2d   "   Wm. G. Hart.
3d   "   Wm. S. McManns.
1st Sergt., Andrew Reed.
2d   "   John McDonagh.
3rd   "   James Doyle.
4th   "   Michael Dnane.
5th   "   Thos. Sweeney (detailed as Right General Guide)
1st Corp'l, Robert McMahon,
2d   "   Chas. Brayton.
3rd   "   James Coyle (left camp at Georgetown on furlough previous to being sworn in, and did not return).
4th   "   John Ward.
5th   "   John Fallon.
1st Drummer, John Hanman.
2d   "   Patrick Coyle.

PRIVATES.

Abraham, George
Ahern, Cornelius
Burns, Maurice
Boyle, John
Burke, Walter
Bolton, G. A.
Brawley, J. N.
Basket, John
Burke. Michael
Bird, P. A.
Conroy, Thomas
Carey, John
Cummings, Christopher

Clark, Edward
Callahan, James
Crystol, Robert
Curry, Hugh
Cunningham, James
Cullene, Patrick
Curran, Peter
Crosby, Michael
Connolly, Thomas
Doheney, Michael
Doheney, Timothy
Doley, James
Dalton, William
Downing, John
Dunnigan, Wm.
Daly, Bernard
Dalton, John
Dugan, John
Fitzgerald, John
Fleming, James
Fleming, Edward
Fromer, George
Finnegan, Theodore
Folk, Daniel W.
Flanigan, John
Fitzgerald, Chas.
Fitchett, R H.
Fallon, Michael
Fitzharris, Edward
Flood, Michael
Gulan, Chas.
Gray, Dan'l J.
Grehey, Patrick
Hoskins, Chas.
Hughes, Thos.
Hughes, Jas.
Hurley, John
Hogan, Michael
Halpin, Jas.
Hackett, John
Indecott, Isaac
Johnson, Robt.
Kating, Michael
Kennedy, George
Kran, Michael
Kingsby, David
King, Timothy
King, Thomas
Kell, Joseph
Karroll, John (detailed as one of the Color Guard).
Kett, Michael
Kearney, Francis
Lowery, Joseph
McNamara, Henry
McKenna, James
McGrane, Patrick
McGrath, Michael
McGrath, Patrick
McGrath, Francis
McGovern, Terence
McCarthy, Felix
McCabe, Patrick
McCabe, Joseph
McKenna, John
McVea, John
Murray, Matthew
Murther, James
Mullavill, John
Martin, Thos.
Murphy, Jos.
Murphy, John
Murray, Michael
Nixon, Peter
Nolan, Lawrence
Nolan, Geo
Nolan, Thos.
O'Connor, Jas.
O'Reilly, Cornelius
O'Brien, Michael
Powers, Wm.
Peetsche, Henry

Purcell, Jas.
Potterton, Jas.
Quinn, Bernard
Quinn, Jas.
Ryan, Jas. De Lacy
Ryan, Jas.—No 1
Ryan, Jas.—No 2
Ryan, Michael T
Rierdon, Daniel
Roach, John
Sayers, Walter
Sinmott, Thos.
Simcox, David
Sweeney, Thomas
Shields, Edward
Sothern, J. S.
Sadlier, Martin
Sheridan, Bryan
Sheeran, Joseph
Tully, Farrell
Tully, Hugh
Ward, Henry
Ward, Joseph
White, Archibald
Walsh, Joseph
Young, John

————

COMPANY F.

Captain, John Breslin.
1st Lieut., Patrick Duffy.
2d   "   Michael Breslin.
3d   "   John H. Nugent.
1st Sergt., Michael Brown.
2d   "   Daniel Taggert.
3d   "   Charles Glynn.
4th   "   Nicholas Judge.
5th   "   David Stephens.
1st Corpl., Nicholas Walsh.
2d   "   James Calhoun.
3d   "   John Fleming.
4th   "   John McGill.
5th   "   Edward McGarry.
1st Musician, Phelim Devitt.
2d   "   James Taggert.

PRIVATES.

Breslin, Patrick
Brady, Bernard
Burns, Henry
Butler, John
Brady, J. Hugh
Cowan, Nicholas
Casey, Patrick
Corcoran, Peter
Carragher, Owen
Coggins, Michael
Casey, John
Cain, Michael
Catles, James
Carr, Thomas
Cunningham, John
Darly, Michael
Darly, William
Daily, Wm.
Dunan, Michael
Donnelly, Patrick
Delaney, Peter
Donahue, Daniel
Draddy, Michael
Davie, Daniel
Dunn, Michael
Dunn, Patrick
Dalton, Edward
Donahue, Alexander
Donahue, Owen
Dogherty, Matthew
Ellingworth, Samuel

Eagen, Robert
Farrell, Joseph
Fallon, John
Fisher, John
Flanigan, Timothy
Foy, William
Froure, Michael
Gallagher, Neil
Gibney, Patrick
Goldrick, Patrick
Howard, Cornelius
Howard, Michael
Hogan, Joseph
Hughes, Francis
Harden, John
Higgins, Chas.
Hawkins, Hugh
Hughes, Patrick
Horan, Patrick
Hilley, Owen
Healey, Thomas
Jordan, F. Thomas
Kelly, John
Keegan, Bernard
Keirnan, Patrick
Kenny, Wm—1st.
Kenny, Wm—2d.
Laffan, Robert
Lyons, Joseph
Lyons, Thomas
McAuliff, James
McAuliff, Patrick
McCabe, Patrick
McDonald, James
McKiernan, John
McKeon, Wm.
McKim, Patrick
McNulty, James
McQuade, Thomas
Mackey, C. John
Maher, Patrick
Marlo, James
Moriarty, John
Morgan, John
Murphy, Francis
Murphy, Michael—1st.
Murphy, Michael—2d.
Murry, Francis
Murry, Timothy
Martagh, Bernard
Nevans, Michael
Nolan, Bernard
O'Brien, Timothy
O'Hara, Michael
O'Neill, Wm.
O'Keefe, Michael
O'Rourke, Michael
Oatis, Patrick
Oliver, Patrick
Parker, S. John
Phife, James
Pidgeon, Christopher
Quin, Michael
Quinn, Timothy
Reardon, Jeremiah
Reilly, Thomas
Ruddrn, Robert
Sullivan, Michael
Seagriff, Lawrence
Snee, Patrick
Silvey, Joseph
Toland, Michael
Tracy, Peter
Telray, Michael
Walsh, Edward
Wooley, Henry

KILLED.

Brady, Patrick

WOUNDED.

Capt. John Breslin (slightly.)
Daily, Michael
Hogan, Joseph (slightly.)
Kenny, Wm —2d.
Nolan, Bernard
McQuade, Thos. (accidentally, while en route from Washington to New York.)

PRISONERS.

Dalton, Edward
Donahue, Owen
Kane, James (wounded.)
Mulany, James (wounded.)
McNulty, James
O'Mally, Dominick (wounded.)

DISCHARGED FOR DISABILITY.

Kennedy, Edward
O'Hara, Philip
O'Rain, Hugh

COMPANY G.

Lieut. Com., Wm. Butler.*
1st Lieut., Henry J. McMahon.
2d   "   Matthew Murphy.
1st Sergt., James McManus.
2d   "   Charles McGuire.
3d   "   James McCream.
4th   "   John McCream.
5th   "   Richard Gallagher.
1st Corpl., Edward Quinn.
2d   "   John Clare.
3d   "   Michael Brennan.
4th   "   Henry P. McGill.
5th   "   Mich. Flannagan.
1st Musician, Thos. Murphy.
2d   "   James Conly.
3d   "   George Phipps.
4th   "   S. Henry.

PRIVATES.

Bannon, Thomas
Brannagan, Thomas
Bernele, Thomas
Barrett, James
Clenery, Robert
Cain, James
Crane, Henry
Cronin, Cornelius
Cabby, Dennis
Cassidy, Daniel
Cronin, Jeremiah
Cornel, Stephen
Campbell, Charles
Core, Thomas
Curley, James
Calhoun, William
Dietich, Valentine
Donoho, Patrick
Donnelly, James
Dunbar, Thomas
Doby, Philip
Fenion, John A.

*Captain Felix Duffy commanded Co. G. until the 17th of May, when he resigned, at Georgetown. First Lieutenant Wm. Butler was ordered to take command of Co. G on the 17th of May, and was its commandant during its term of service.

Flemming, Thomas
Flanigan, James
Flynn, Owen
Flynn, Patrick
Fox, John
Gafney, Patrick
Gallagher, George
Gallagher. James
Geehan, Michael
Gill, Matthew
Genan, Michael
Godfrey, William
Griffin, Patrick
Guy, William
Hinton, Johnston
Higgins. Henry
Hobin, Joseph
Hanlon, James
Harrington, Timothy
Hara, Thomas
Haley, Martin
Hogan, Thomas
Holland, Nicholas
Howard. John
Jones, David
Kennedy, John
Lavelle, Hugh
Leahey, Jeremiah
Lennon, William
Little, John
Lynes, Maurice
Lynes, Michael
Loftus, Peter
Maloney. Patrick
Marley, Michael
Martin, James
Mahoney. Maurice
Martin, Bernard
Margrand, Patrick
Meagher, Stephen
Meehan, David
Moon, Terrance
Moran, John
Middleton, William
McCarthy, Daniel
McCarthy, Patrick B.
McCarthy, John
McElhoney, Patrick
McCullough, James
McConnell, Philip
McDonald, Martin
McDonald, Daniel
McGill, Patrick
McDonagh, Patrick
McGurn, John
McGuinness
McHugh, William P.
McWickle, Thomas
McElroy, Arthur
Murphy, James
Murray, Patrick J.
Malvey, John
Mullins, Thomas
Mulvey, Thomas
Neville, Dennis
O'Brien, Edward
O'Brien, James
O'Brien, John
O'Brien, Francis
O'Neill, James
O'Sullivan, Lawrence
O'Brien, Thomas
Powers, Francis
Quinn, George
Scanlan, James
Shea, John
Sullivan, Maurice
Sullivan, Dennis
Trainor, Francis
Tullerey, Dennis
Touhey, James
Vaughan, John

Wheeling, Thomas
Wallace, Richard
Walsh, Michael
Whelan, Matthew

KILLED

Flynn, P. H.
Higgins, Anthony
Flemming, Thomas (accidentally, on the railroad coming toward Philadelphia).

WOUNDED.

Lieut. Butler, slightly, in the shoulder.
Michael Brennan, 3d Corporal
James Curley
James Gallagher.
John McCream, 4th Sergeant.
James Hanlon.
Michael Holland.
McGill.
McNichol.
Rubey.
Richard.
Thomas M. Resby.
Richard Wallace.

MISSING.

Stephen Connor.
John Vaughan (died in hospital).
Michael Brennan, wounded.
Donnelly.
Thomas Dunbar.

DESERTED.

Sergt. Philip McConnell.
Corporal Thomas Punk.
Slempecker Henry, musician.
P. R. J. Murray and John McGuire, privates.

COMPANY H.*

Captain, James Kelly.
1st Lieut., William Butler, detailed to the command of Co. G.
2d Lieut., J. Gannon, a prisoner.
3d Lieut., J. Lowery.
1st Sergt., Robert Callaghan.
2d   "   Michael Lowery.
3d   "   Patrick Mahon.
4th   "   James Poley.
1st Corpl., Terence Scanlan.
2d   "   Cornelius O'Keefe.
3d   "   John McManus.
4th   "   Daniel Hogan.
5th   "   James Dolan.
Drummer, William William.

PRIVATES.

Adams, William
Hulbert, John
Burns, Richard
Bulger, John
Berry, Thomas
Brown, Thomas
Bulger, Peter
Burke, Michael
Bunnan, John

* Extracted from the Paymaster's Roll—no other source of information being available.

Burey, Charles
Brady, Terence
Brennan, Luke
Callaghan, Patrick
Curren, Martin
Coonan, James
Cronan, John
Coonan, John
Collins, Jeremiah
Conroy, Thomas
Curliss, Paul
Callaghan, Michael
Carrol, George
Cunningham, Patrick
Cavannagh, Patrick
Cavannagh, Peter
Campbell, Henry
Campbell Samuel
Carney, Patrick
Crossin, Authority
Doran, John
Duffy, Patrick E.
Egan, David
Foley, Michael
Flannelly, Michael
Fagan, William
Fitzgerald, Cornelius
Gibney, Thomas
Grant, George
Gegety, Matthew
Gilroy, Peter
Gorman, Michael
Howe, William G.
Higgins, Thomas
Hayes, Michael
Hammell, Owen
Jennings, Thomas
Kelly, Patrick
Kelly, Frederick
King, Patrick
Keenan. Matthew
Linaghan, Matthew
McCarthy, Charles
Maher, Patrick
Morris, John
Marra, Thos.
Markey, John
Mulloy, Matthew
McCormick, M. J.
Marrion, James
McManus, Daniel
McGuire, Michael
McGahan, James
McCann, John
McCann. Peter
McDonald, Matthew
Madden, James
McMahon, Michael
McGrath, Joseph
McCarthy, Thomas
McManus, John
Madden, Denis
Manen, Thomas
Muney, Edward
Mitchell, Dennis
McEvoy, Bernard
Mulrooney, Richard
Murley, Francis
Nelson, Thomas
Nolan, Michael
O'Brien, John
O'Brien, Denis J.
O'Connor, Daniel
O'Sullivan, John
O'Sullivan, Michael
Parker, Robert
Perkins, Edward
Reily, Charles
Ryan, Daniel J.
Reily, Patrick
Reynolds, James
Rice, Henry

Ryan, John
Reardon, Charles
Shirlock, Augustus
Shew, H. Lewis
Tierny, Thomas
Topey, Patrick
Tehan, John
William, David
Wynne, Patrick R.
White, Nicholas

COMPANY I.

1st Lieut. Commanding, John Coonan.
2d Lieut., Thomas M'Canton.
3d   "   William Fogarty.
1st Sergt., Thomas Scanlon.
2d   "   John Joseph Foster.
3d   "   Patrick Morris.
4th   "   John Gleeson.
5th   "   Meagher.*
1st Corp'l, Thos. Donoghue.
2d   "   James Watson.
3d   "   Jeremiah Preston.
4th   "   James McGowan.
5th   "   Patrick O'Connor.
DRUMMER, Richard Conroy.

PRIVATES.

Barney, Matthew
Bates, Hugh
Bagley, Peter
Bartley, William
Bergen, Thomas
Bell, Christopher
Bird, Laurence
Bowes, John
Brett, Denis
Brien, Michael J.
Britten, Edward
Brown, John
Brothwell, John
Byrne, Edward
Cahill, Thomas
Callaghan, Bartholemew
Callaghan, James, 1st
Callahan, James, 2d
Canton, Joseph
Carley, Patrick
Cleary, Michael
Connor, Philip
Cosgrove, Patrick
Coats, Michael
Comfort, Matthew
Connor, James
Coss, Kiernan
Croker, Walter
Crogan, Thomas
Curry, Charles
Daly, John
Daly, Matthew
Daly, Michael
Delany, William
Divine, Richard
Divine, Alexander
Divine, Thomas
Dempsey, Peter J.
Disney, George M.
Doyle, Edward
Duggan, Cornelius
Dumphey, Patrick

* This man was not heard of after the encounter with the enemy on the Thursday previous to the battle at Bull Run, and is supposed to have deserted.

Dolan, Thomas
Donnelly, John
Eagan, Daniel
Emmett, John
Fitzgerald, Cornelius
Folis, Edward
Fullham, Michael
Franklin, James
Gallagher, Christopher
Geary, Jeremiah
Giddings, John
Gillan, Michael
Gillespie, Hugh
Haffey, Patrick
Hale, Bernard
Hagem, John
Hurley, John
Irwin, James
Jackson, Joseph
Jacques, John
Kelly, Peter
King, Charles
Kinnealy, William
Lalor, John P.
Lalor, Jeremiah
Leonard, Edward
Lovett, Christopher
Lynch, John
Lynch, Patrick
Lynch, Richard
Madden, James
Maddigan, Thomas
McCarty, Daniel
McGee, Daniel
McGee, Richard
McGowan, John
McCan, John
McGrane, Francis
McGrane, Michael
McGrane, Patrick
McMahon, John W.
McGirk, Andrew
Molloy, George
Mullany, John
Mulligan, Michael   *
Murphy, Daniel
Murphy, John
Murphy, Thomas
Nesbitt, James
Neugent, Lawrence
Norris, Richard
O'Brie, Michael
O'Dea, James
O'Donnell, Patrick
O'Neill, John
O'Reilly, Thomas D.
O'Reilly, Patrick
Palmer, John
Perkins, Matthew
Philbin, Patrick
Ponton, Robert
Powers, John
Pryor, Ferguson
Quinn, John
Rowan, John
Ryan, Daniel
Ryan, Joseph
Smith, Henry
Smith, James
Smith, Peter
Sullivan, James, 1st
Sullivan, James, 2d
Sexton, Patrick
Shannon, Patrick
Stencune, John
Scanlan, Joseph
Sheehan, Cornelius
Sheehan, John
Venus, John I.*

* The only Englishman by birth in the regiment.

KILLED.

Brothwell, John
Kelly, Peter
Smith, Peter
Sullivan, James, 1st

PRISONERS AT RICHMOND.

Captain James McIver. This gentleman joined the regiment as a private at Washington, and a fortnight before his arrest was elected Captain of Company I.

COMPANY K.

(IRISH ZOUAVES.)

Captain, T. F. Meagher.
1st Lieut., E. K. Butler.
2d   "   Maurice M. Wall.
3d   "   Edmund Connolly.
1st Sergt., Wm. O'Donohue.
2d   "   Jos. T. M. Kelly.
3d   "   Michael Kennelly.
4th   "   John Breslin.
5th   "   William Hogan.
1st Corpl., Joseph O'Donohue.
2d   "   John Hillulpen.
3d   "   Chas O'Neill.
4th   "   Hubert M. Irwin.
5th   "   J. O'Connell Joyce.
1st Drummer, D. Connolly.
2d   "   Edward Walsh.

PRIVATES.

Agnew, Daniel
Ahern, Cornelius
Annesly, Wm.
Barrett, Jas. Joseph
Burke, Dennis
Brown, Francis
Blake, John
Byron, John W.
Beaty, Patrick
Byrne, James

Barry, James
Byrne, Thos. Jas.
Cassidy, Daniel
Clarke, John C.
Callahan, Wm.
Clooney, P. F.
Cronan, Timothy
Coll, Patrick
Clarke, Thomas
Costello, James
Connerty, Michael
Condon, John
Curry, Michael
Collins, Daniel
Collins, Raymond H.
Cummings, Wm.
Carsy, Thomas
Coyle, Charles
Duffy, James
Dowd, Alexander
Dolphin, Matthew J.
Dalton, William
Dunphy, John J.
Devin, William
Doyle, James
Devine, James
Eagan, William
Fean, John
Finn, James D.
Finnen, Richard
Fitzgerald, Thomas F.
Flagherty, Thomas
Geany, John
Hayes, Thomas
Healy, Patrick
Healy, Thomas
Healy, Wm.
Horan, John
Hughes, Thomas K.
Hurly, John C.
Kavenagh, John H.
Kavenagh, Thomas J.
Kane, James
Kelly, Daniel
Kelly, Edward
Keenan, Michael
Keyes, Joseph
Keely, Patrick

King, Martin
Kirwin, Edward
Ledwich, John
Lynch, John
Mahady, Daniel E.
Maginn, Patrick
McClosky, Thomas
McCarthy, Owen
McDonald, James
McGoey, John C.
McQuinn, Michael
Mortugh, James
Meagher, James
Mannix, Michael
Mullins, Chas.
Mullins, William
Morris, William
McGuire, John C.
O'Brien, James
O'Brien, Patrick
O'Brien, Wm. McMahon
O'Connor, Chas.
O'Connor, Patrick
O'Connor, Wm. R.
O'Keefe, John D.
O'Keefe, Michael
O'Meara, Patrick
O'Niel, Richard
Powers, John
Qname, Pierce F.
Rivly, John
Rieley, Owen
Rielly, Chas.
Ryan, John
Ryan, Philip J.
Shaughnessy, Edward
Smith, John
Sparks, John
Spencer, Wm.
Stanley, Thomas
Taylor, Robert
Toland, Edward
Tracy, Jeremiah
Warran, Stephen
Webster, John
White, Geo. E.
Whitty, William
Williams, Chas.

PEACE AND VICTORY!

FUNSTON & SCOFIELD, 62 JOHN STREET.

There is not a loyal man throughout the length and breadth of the land who is not persuaded in his own mind that ere the fall fully sets in, Seccessionism, and with it every trace of rebellion, will be banished from the south. As this most welcome period will be ushered in with great rejoicing, we beg to remind the reader that among those who contribute to the joyous hilarity of festive seasons is the respected firm of Messrs. FUNSTON & SCOFIELD, sole agents for Mr. LILLIENDAHL, that eminent manufacturer of Pyrotechnics. They are constantly supplied with all descriptions of Fire Works. Some of the designs of this establishment have earned for them a reputation of excellence which may be imitated but cannot be surpassed. From the extensive character of Mr. Lilliendahl's establishment, Messrs. Funston & Scofield are prepared at all times to fill orders, and to execute designs with promptness and dispatch. Remember their address,

62 JOHN STREET, NEW-YORK.

A SEASONABLE AND A HEALTHY BEVERAGE.

Of the various descriptions and qualities of Ale now produced and put upon the market, that known as "Flemming's Golden Ale" stands the foremost, and as its excellent qualities become more known, it is more and more in demand, and universally appreciated. That we do not exaggerate in the classification of this article, is demonstrated by the fact that the "Golden Ale" has obtained several first class medals at the State fairs in New-York, the judges pronouncing it in every instance composed of the purest ingredients. Chemical analysists give it as their opinion that this Ale is a decidedly healthy beverage, and such as should find its way into private families. It is already sold in wood and in bottles in all the first-class hotels and saloons in this city and throughout the country. Its excellent quality for keeping at sea renders it desirable for shipping and ship stores. PIERCE SKEHAN, sole Agent for this Ale, has his Depot at 158 BROADWAY, where it can be had wholesale and retail, in bottle and in wood. We cordially recommend Flemming's Golden Ale, and advise purchasers to give Mr. Skehan a call.

PROSPECTUS

OF THE

CHRONICLES OF THE REBELLION

OF 1861.

————————

THE undersigned has the pleasure of intimating that he has made arrangements for publishing, in Weekly Parts, of Twenty-Four Pages Octavo, Price Ten Cents, a a work entitled as above.

"The Chronicles of the Rebellion of 1861"

Will form a complete History of the Secession movement from its commencement, and contain every fact and incident of interest during the campaign.

SKETCHES OF THE LIVES OF THE LEADING GENERALS NORTH AND SOUTH

will be given, and an epitome of all the State and National Documents relating to the great struggle.

To render the work a standard of reference in all coming time, it is the intention of the undersigned to give in each part

THE MUSTER ROLL OF ONE REGIMENT,

who volunteered to fight the battles of their country, and maintain, inviolate, the honor and dignity of our National Flag, and the supremacy of the Constitution and Laws of the United States. Each Muster Roll will be preceded by a narrative of the march of such regiment from its place of enrolment to the seat of hostilities; noting with fidelity every occurence worthy of mention, and recording every act of devoted loyalty and heroism from the colonel down to the humblest private.

THE MUSTER ROLL OF THE SIXTY-NINTH REGIMENT, N. Y. S. M.,

WILL BE GIVEN IN THE SECOND PART, WHICH WILL APPEAR AUGUST 17.

Determined to spare neither pains nor expense, the undersigned hopes to produce a historic work, which will find its way into every dwelling throughout the land. Great care will be taken in the Literary Department, and the Typography and Paper shall be of the best class. To all who desire to possess a full and unbiassed description of the crisis invoked by secession, this book will be without a compeer, whilst its moderate price brings it within the reach of the poorest of our citizens.

A limited number of Advertisements will be published on the covers, at moderate charges.

CHARLES J. ROSS,

EDITOR AND PROPRIETOR.

New-York, 1861.

PEACE AND VICTORY

FUNSTON & SCOFIELD, 62 JOHN STREET.

There is not a loyal man throughout the length and breadth of the land who is not persuaded in his own mind that ere the fall fully sets in, Seccessionism, and with it every trace of rebellion, will be banished from the south. As this most welcome period will be ushered in with great rejoicing, we beg to remind the reader that among those who contribute to the joyous hilarity of festive seasons is the respected firm of Messrs. FUNSTON & SCOFIELD, sole agents for Mr. LILLIENDAHL, that eminent manufacturer of Pyrotechnics. They are constantly supplied with all descriptions of Fire Works. Some of the designs of this establishment have earned for them a reputation of excellence which may be imitated but cannot be surpassed. From the extensive character of Mr. Lilliendahl's establishment, Messrs. Funston & Scofield are prepared at all times to fill orders, and to execute designs with promptness and dispatch. Remember their address,

62 JOHN STREET, NEW-YORK.

A Seasonable and a Healthly Beverage !

Of the various descriptions and qualities of Ale now produced and put upon the market, that known as "Flemming's Golden Ale" stands the foremost, and as its excellent qualities become more known, it is more and more in demand, and univer ally appreciated. That we do not exaggerate in the clasification of this article, is demonstrated by the fact that the "Golden Ale" has obtained several first class medals at the State fairs in New-York, the judges pronouncing it in every instance composed of the purest ingredients. Chemical analysists give it as their opinion that this Ale is a decidedly healthy beverage, and such as should find its way into private families. It is already sold in wood and in bottles in all the first-class hotels and saloons in this city and throughout the country. Its excellent quality for keeping at sea renders it desirab'e for shipping and ship stores. PIERCE SKEHAN, sole Agent for this Ale, has his depot at 158 BROADWAY, where it can be had wholesale and retail, in bottle and in wood. We cordially recommend Flemming's Golden Ale, and advise purchasers to give Mr. Skehan a call.

ADVERTISEMENTS.

DANIEL CUNNINGHAM,
WHOLESALE AND RETAIL DEALER IN
FOREIGN & DOMESTIC
WINES, LIQUORS & SEGARS,
No. 11 James Street,

Corner of New Bowery,　　　　　　　NEW YORK.

WILLIAM BUTLER,
CHOICE WINES, LIQUORS & SEGARS,
No. 193 AVENUE B,

Corner of 12th Street.　　　　　　　NEW-YORK.

PETER McQUADE,
WINE & SPIRIT MERCHANT,

Liquors of all kinds, and Cigars of the choicest quality at lowest prices,

STORES, 26 CANAL AND 14 ANN STS.

GREAT REDUCTION IN THE PRICE OF

SINGER & CO'S STANDARD MACHINES,

WELL KNOWN TO BE THE BEST FOR MANUFACTURING PURPOSES:

No. 1, Standard Shuttle Machine, formerly sold at $90, Reduced to $70.

No. 2,   "   "   " formerly sold at $100, Reduced to $75.

SINGER'S LETTER A. MACHINE

Is the best Machine in the world for FAMILY SEWING and LIGHT MANUFACTURING PURPOSES: Price, (*with Hemmer*,) and beautifully ornamented, **$50.**

The Nos. 1 and 2 Machines are of great capacity and application for manufacturing purposes.

Our No. 3 Machines are especially adapted to all kinds of light and heavy Leather Work, in Carriage Trimming, Boot and Shoe Making, Harness Making, etc., etc. They are of extra size, with an arm long enough to take under it and stitch the largest size dashes. There is scarcely any part of a Trimmers' stitching that cannot be better done with them than by hand ; so, too, the saving of time and labor is very great. The table of these Machines is 24 inches long, and the shuttle will hold six times the usual quantity of thread. The large machines work as last as small ones.

We would ask for our Letter A Machines, the special attention of Vest Makers and Dress Makers, and all those who want Machines for *light manufacturing purposes*. They embody the principles of the standard machines, making like them, the interlocked stitch, and are destined to be as celebrated for FAMILY SEWING and *light* manufacturing purposes as our standard machines are for manufacturing purposes in general.

We have always on hand, **HEMMING GUAGES, SILK TWIST, LINEN & COTTON THREAD, ON SPOOLS, BEST MACHINE OIL IN BOTTLES, ETC., ETC.**

We manufacture our own Needles, and would warn all persons using our machines not to buy any others. We know that there are needles sold *of the most inferior quality*, at higher prices than we charge for the best. The needles sold by us are manufactured especially for our machines. *A bad needle may render the best machine almost useless.*

Our customers may rest assured that all our Branch Offices are furnished with the "genuine article."

In case of small purchases, the money may be sent in postage stamps, or bank notes.

☞ Correspondents will please write their names distinctly. It is all important that we should, in each case, know the Post Office, County and State.

☞ We have made the above REDUCTION IN PRICES with the two-fold view of benefiting the public and ourselves. The public have been swindled by spurious machines made in imitation of ours. The metal in them, from the iron casting to the smallest piece, is of poor quality. Their makers have not the means to do the work well. They are hid away in secret places, where it would be impossible to have at their command the proper mechanical appliances. It is only by doing a great business, and having extensive manufacturing establishments, that good machines can be made at moderate prices. The best designed machines, BADLY MADE, are always liable to get out of order, and are sure to cost considerable trouble and money to keep them in repair.

The qualities to be looked for in a Machine are : *certainty of correct action at all rates of speed, simplicity of construction, great durability, and rapidity of operation, with the least labor.* Machines to combine these essential qualities, must be made of the *best metal* and *finished to perfection.* We have the ways and means, on a grand scale, to do this.

The purchasers of Machines, whose daily bread it may concern, will find that those having the above qualities not only work well at *rapid* as well as *slow* rates of speed, but *last long* in the finest possible working order. Our machines, *as made by us*, will earn *more money* with *less labor* than any others whether in imitation of ours or not. In fact, they are cheaper than any other machines as a gift.

I. M. SINGER & CO., 458 Broadway, New York.

DR. R. F. HIBBARD'S WILD CHERRY BITTERS

For Nervous Weakness and General Debility.

These celebrated Bitters, which have stood the test of years, are invaluable in the cure of all bilious complaints, such as fever and ague, jaundice, bilious colic, flatulence and dyspepsia, also palpitation of the heart, and dizziness of the head, as well as in the hectic fever of scrofula and consumption. This medicine is not only a tonic, but is also a sedative, or an anti-spasmodic, and has a tendency to allay nervous irritations and excitability.

THE WILD CHERRY BITTERS ARE PREPARED BY

RUFUS F. HIBBARD, No. 102 FULTON STREET, NEW YORK,

PRICE 50 CENTS AND $1 PER BOTTLE.

The following well-known remedies can also be obtained at 102 Fulton Street—

Rev. B. Hibbard's Anti-Bilious Family Pills................12½ and 25 cents per box.
R. F. Hibbard's Circassian Balm.....................25 cts. per bottle.
      Coloris Capilli Restitutor...........................$1   "
      Rheumatic Lotion ....25 cts.   "
Rev. B. Hibbard's Carminative Salve................................25 cts.   "

All the above manufactured and sold, wholesale and retail, by

R. F. HIBBARD, 102 Fulton Street, New-York.

BRADY'S
Seventh Regiment Gymnasium,

Entrance, No. 20 ST. MARK'S PLACE, (8th STREET.)

The Seventh Regiment Gymnasium is now open to the public.

TERMS.

$16 00..**Per Year.**
10 00..**Six months.**
7 00..**Three Months.**

Which entitles the subscriber to the free use of the Gymnasium, Running Track, Parlors, Reading, Billiards, and Chess Rooms, Hot and Cold Baths, and locker with key, &c.

No extra charge for joining the Classes.

Gentlemen are invited to call and inspect the institution.

ABNER S. BRADY, Proprietor.

A. S B. will personally attend Classes in Calesthenics and Gymnastics in Schools, Colleges, &c.

A CERTAIN CURE FOR THE PILES!

A Novelty in the Medical World!

PIERCY'S PATENT PILE PIPE.

AND PILE OINTMENT!

This Pipe, recently patented, is an entirely new invention, being a mechanical contrivance for the more convenient and complete application of curative, sedative and lubricating ointment, in the treatment of Piles and other diseases of the rectum : and for these objects it is unsurpassed in simplicity, cleanliness and efficiency of operation. The patient can use it himself without assistance, and children can readily understand it and use it without help.

It is invaluable in all diseases where applications or injections are required, but in the treatment of Piles especially, with the proper ointments. The most beneficial results have followed in every instance. Cases of long standing, after trying every other known remedy, and in some instances pronounced hopeless, have experienced immediate relief, and have ultimately been cured.

Testimonials from Physicians and others who have used the Pipe can be seen at the office of the undersigned.

PRICE OF PIPE $3.

A liberal discount made to Physicians, Druggists, and wholesale and retail dealers generally.

ADDRESS, **HENRY R. PIERCY,**

102 Fulton St., N. Y., and 5 Willoughby St., Brooklyn

THE PATRIOT'S REFEREE;
CONTAINING THE

Declaration of Independence, the Original Articles of Confederation, the Constitution of the United States, and Washington's Farewell Address.

ALL COMPLETE. AFFORDING TO EVERY ONE A MEANS OF REFERENCE AT ONCE RELIABLE AND CONVENIENT.

Address, Box 175, P. O., N. Y. **E. N. CARVALHO, Publisher.**

CHRONICLES OF THE REBELLION

OF 1861

"The Chronicles of the Rebellion of 1861"

www.ingramcontent.com/pod-product-compliance
Lightning Source LLC
Chambersburg PA
CBHW021522090426
42739CB00007B/729